Captains from Devon

You Gentlemen of England,
  that live at home at ease,
Full little do you think upon
  the Dangers of the Seas:
Give ear unto the Marriners,
  and they will plainly show
The cares and the fears
  when the stormy winds do blow.

　　　· · ·

We bring home costly merchandise,
  and Jewels of great price,
To serve our *English* Gallantry
  with many a rare device:
To please the *English* Gallantry
  Our pains we freely show,
For we toyl and we woyl,
  when the stormy winds do blow.

From "Neptune's Raging Fury,
or the Gallant Seaman's Sufferings"
(A 16th-century sea ballad)

Queen Elizabeth I, the "Armada" portrait.

Captains from Devon

THE GREAT ELIZABETHAN SEAFARERS
WHO WON THE OCEANS
FOR ENGLAND

Helen Hill Miller

Algonquin Books
of Chapel Hill
1985

Algonquin Books of Chapel Hill
Post Office Box 2225
Chapel Hill, North Carolina 27515–2225

LIBRARY OF CONGRESS CATALOGING IN PUBLICATION DATA

Miller, Helen Hill, 1899–
Captains from Devon.

Includes index.
1. Great Britain—History, Naval—Tudors, 1485–1603.
2. Navigation—Great Britain—History—16th century.
I. Title.
DA86.M55   1985   942.05   85-15712
ISBN 0-912697-27-X

Printed in the United States of America

Contents

Illustrations

Author's Note

In 1582, Pope Gregory XIII instituted a new calendar that would more accurately measure the annual orbit of the earth around the sun. Catholic countries in Europe readily adopted the pope's reform; Protestant England did not. By tradition, the dating of events in English history follows the Julian calendar up until the middle of the eighteenth century, when England at last accepted the calendar used everywhere today. Thus all of the dates given in this account of the great Elizabethan seafarers are "Old Style." Here, for example, the date of the Battle of Gravelines is as the English marked it: July 29, 1588; in an account from the Spanish point of view, the date would be given as August 8.

Another matter of style also bears mention. The English in Elizabeth I's day allowed for considerable variation in the spelling of words, including names. In most instances, I have used modern spellings for the names of key figures in the story I have to tell. However, I have omitted the "i" in Sir Walter Ralegh's name. He himself usually wrote it as it appears in this text.

Captains from Devon

A Gentle Knight was pricking on the plaine,
    Ycladd in mightie armes and silver shielde,
    Wherein old dints of deepe wounds did remaine,
    The cruell markes of many a bloudy fielde;
    Yet armes till that time did he never wield:
    His angry steede did chide his foming bitt,
    As much disdayning to the curbe to yield:
    Full jolly knight he seemed, and faire did sitt,
As one for knightly giusts and fierce encounters fitt.

. . .

Upon a great adventure he was bond,
    That greatest *Gloriana* to him gave,
    That greatest Glorious Queene of *Faerie* Lond,
    To winne him worship, and her grace to have,
    Which of all earthly things he most did crave;
    And ever as he rode, his hart did earne
    To prove his puissance in battell brave
    Upon his foe, and his new force to learne;
Upon his foe, a Dragon horrible and stearne.

Edmund Spenser, *The Faerie Queene* (Bk. I, canto 1, stanzas 1 & 3)

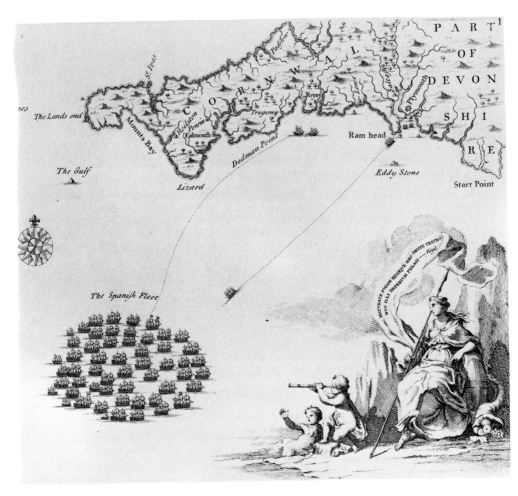

Route of Capt. John Fleming as he returned to Plymouth after sighting many Spanish galleons hulled down south of the Lizard.

I

Challenge to Gloriana

NTIL MID-AFTERNOON, JULY 19, 1588, WAS JUST
another Friday on Plymouth's waterfront. All day, loading
and unloading had gone forward at the wharfsides of the
quiet pool above the barbican. Idlers observing ships entering and leaving port casually noticed that Captain John Fleming was
coming in; his vessel was one of a number that were taking turns
patrolling the western entrance to the Channel. They kept watch off The
Lizard, the southern point of the double-tipped peninsula that forms
Land's End in Cornwall.

But Captain Fleming, who had just covered some ninety sea miles to
bring the news, had aboard a momentous message. As he jumped from
his boat and started up the steep slope from the harbor to the flat high
land of Plymouth Hoe, the words he tossed over his shoulder spread in
quick circles.

He was looking for Charles, Lord Howard of Effingham, Queen
Elizabeth's Lord High Admiral, commander of the English fleet. By-
standers on the wharf thought Lord Howard might be enjoying an
afternoon game up at the bowling greens. Fleming's message: the long-
awaited Spanish Armada had arrived! In the stretch of water south of the
Scilly Isles, a gathering of great galleons had been sighted, hulled down,
apparently waiting for more to arrive. They could now be as close as a
day's sail.

Howard had recently divided the queen's ships into two stout squadrons, leaving one in the east to guard the Kentish coast and the seaway up
the Thames estuary; he himself had come to join the other, stationed at
Plymouth to withstand the initial impact of the enemy.

On arrival, he had presented Sir Francis Drake with the flag of the
fleet's vice admiral. Drake was in his home port, and so was John
Hawkins, relieved of Navy Board duties to serve as the fleet's rear admiral, third in overall command.

Among all the English captains, Drake's was the name that Spain most feared: El Draque, the circumnavigator; El Draque, the ravaging pirate in the Caribbean; El Draque, intrepid spoiler of home ports along the Portuguese and Spanish coasts; El Draque, the dragon whose raid on Cadiz the previous year destroyed so much shipping that he upset King Philip's schedule for the start of his Enterprise of England.

Other major members of Devon's marine confraternity were on duty on land. Some months before, Elizabeth's favorite courtier, Sir Walter Ralegh, and Sir Richard Grenville, who had captained the fleet that brought the first English-speaking colonists to the mid-Atlantic coast of North America in 1585, had been assigned to strengthen England's south-coast defenses lest the Spaniards try to secure a port for a naval base or a beachhead for invasion there. And from early spring, Plymouth's seventy-year-old mayor, for thirty years head of the Hawkins family's famous firm of Plymouth merchants, shipowners, and shipbuilders, had overseen the putting of the western squadron into top condition for action.

To these men, Captain Fleming's news had only tactical importance: everyone knew that a contest between England and Spain was on the way. War had indeed been growing in likelihood for thirty years, ever since Protestant Elizabeth succeeded Catholic Mary on the English throne; it had been imminent ever since diplomatic relations between the two powers were broken in 1585. On the next day, July 20, when a great sweep of Spanish men-of-war, propelled by a propitious wind, was silhouetted blackly against the western horizon, the rumors that Philip had built a fleet of hitherto unseen proportions were all too awesomely confirmed. Since the Armada, if it had followed a course closer to the south shore of the Channel, could have remained for some time un-observed from English shores, its choice of early recognition may have been a deliberate decision to emphasize its enormous majesty.

The contemporary artists' renderings of the Armada's advance, shown in the illustrations of Chapter VI, display it as a great close-packed half-moon; but, looking at these pictures, practical-minded navigators sus-pect that ships so tightly gathered would have robbed each other of wind. The name "half-moon" may have been given by landsmen looking

Artists portrayed the Spanish order of battle as a half-moon.

down on the spectacle from English clifftops; once given, however inaccurate, it stuck. Sir Walter Ralegh, in his treatise on *The Art of War at Sea*, observed that "To clap ships together, without consideration, belongs rather to a mad man, than to a man of warre: . . . In like sort had the Lord Charles Howard, Admirall of England, beene lost in the yeere 1588 if he had not beene better advised, than a great many malignant fooles were, that found fault with his demeanour." But the actual formation was quite as intimidating—the distance between ship and ship was said to be only fifty paces—and even witnesses who knew their ropes were filled with something like the landlubbers' amazement. From tip to tip, Spain's entering wedge spread over two miles of sea.

Causes for the coming conflict had been long accumulating. The old saying that trade follows the flag can be quite as true if reversed. In the days when the flags of western European powers were being planted on far-off soil, the voyages that took their mariners to newly discovered places were being urged upon their sovereigns and often organized, financed, and dispatched by merchant traders eager for access to distant goods.

For more than a century, pent-up pressure to locate a sea route to the Orient had stimulated ocean ventures. Historically, overland camel caravans had trodden the thousands of miles of the Silk Road, transporting spices, silks, pearls, and other luxuries from China to Mediterranean shores. But with the rise of new Turkish empires, their Middle Eastern termini had been blocked. Thus deprived, western Europeans had become impatient for spices to improve the winter palatability of long-stored meat and fish.

The Portuguese were the first to find a way. Around 1420, Prince Henry the Navigator, a scholar absorbed in geography and seamanship, set up a school of navigation at Sagres, on the tip of his country's southwest peninsula, and little by little induced mariners to venture down the West African coast. By the end of the fifteenth century, Vasco da Gama had rounded the Cape of Good Hope and opened for Portugal a sea route to the Orient unchallenged by any other power.

Though sailing out of sight of land was still unfamiliar, its danger was mitigated in the Indian Ocean because the steady, regular, seasonal monsoons could be relied on to propel ships back and forth between Madagascar and India. During the summer months, the monsoon blew steadily from the southwest; then, in the following season, it conveniently reversed direction. One could traverse the route almost without a touch on the tiller. From bases in India, Portuguese seamen could follow the coasts east toward the Spice Islands (the Moluccas) and north to China.

Spain was the next overseas venturer. In 1492, the persistent Genoese sailor Christopher Columbus finally secured Ferdinand and Isabella's sponsorship for his project of reaching India by sailing directly west.

Naves e China et Iava velis ex arundine
contextis et anchoris ligneis.

Schepen van China en Iava met rietten
seylen en houten anckers

32 m 33

Sixteenth-century merchandising in the Orient.

What he actually found were the offshore islands of an unsuspected landmass, but he opened the way to a gold-bearing conquest.

Between them, the Iberian countries then controlled the riches of an expanding world. In 1493, Pope Alexander VI initiated formal division of the newfound lands between these two Catholic powers, expressed by them in the Treaty of Tordesillas, along a north-south line of demarcation in the Atlantic Ocean 370 leagues west of the Cape Verde Islands; all newly discovered territory to the east of it was Portugal's, all to the west, Spain's.

In the course of these events, England's position on greatly revised world maps underwent dramatic change. Previously, all charts were Mediterranean-centered; Elizabeth's kingdom appeared merely as half of a far western offshore island. Only uncharted ocean was shown beyond it, balancing sketchy renditions of the Orient in the extreme east; northern or southern areas at any distance above or below Mediterranean shores were frankly labeled *terra incognita*. But by the time Elizabeth's reign was over, Shakespeare, in his *King John*, vaunted a new position for

> . . . that whitefac'd shore,
> Whose foot spurns back the ocean's roaring tides
> And coops from other lands her islanders,
> . . . that England, hedg'd in with the main,
> That water-walled bulwark, still secure
> And confident from foreign purposes . . .

From the mid-sixteenth century on, up-to-date maps—and the newly invented globes—filled empty spaces with verified outlines, and many ocean charts exhibited dotted lines of trade routes or famous voyages.

England first attempted to locate a seaway of her own to the Far East in a passage above northern Europe. Just before Elizabeth's accession, merchant adventurers had financed several probes in that direction. By extension of traditional coastal sailing, the voyages of Sir William Willoughby and Richard Chancellor and their successors opened up trade with Russia, but they did not disclose a complete Northeast Passage: their ships were remorselessly blocked by ice. Once this attempt and a similar effort over North America were abandoned, the alternative was to sail out into territories claimed by the pope's assignees. Only so could England put her mark on the new geography and become a world power.

The situation required a daunting reversal of foreign policy. England's hereditary enemy had been France. As recently as 1545, an imposing French fleet had appeared off the Isle of Wight, bent on invasion. Former rule of French territory was symbolized on the English royal blazon where fleur-de-lys were quartered along with the royal lions; the nation still smarted at the extinguishment of the last bit of English sovereignty on French soil by the loss of Calais in 1558, only months before Elizabeth became ruler.

Until Elizabeth's reign, Tudor England had balanced and encircled

French power by forming Continental alliances with Habsburg monarchs and princes of the Holy Roman Empire. Henry VIII's first wife was the Spanish princess Catherine of Aragon, youngest daughter of Their Catholic Majesties, Ferdinand and Isabella; she became the mother of Mary, queen of England from 1553 to 1558. In 1556 Mary's consort, the Spanish prince Philip, succeeded to the throne of Spain as King Philip II; for the remaining two years of her life, the husband of England's queen ruled England's chief ally. When Philip's father, the Holy Roman Emperor Charles V, abdicated his worldly titles during 1555–56, preparatory to entering a monastery, France was surrounded by his progeny: his sons and other relatives ruled Spain, Portugal, Austria, various German and Italian principalities, the holdings of the Burgundian dukes, and the southern parts of the Netherlands.

In the Netherlands, Spanish rule had proved difficult: the northwestern provinces of Holland and Zeeland remained in open and successful revolt, Catholic and Protestant divisions were sharp, and distaste for a more unified government than the states-general of the federated provinces persisted. But by 1585, the superb and exacting generalship of Philip II's nephew, Alessandro Farnese, duke of Parma, had consolidated Spanish power in the southern Low Countries, the area of Belgium today.

As heir to a foreign policy of French containment, Elizabeth could not fail to look upon cancellation of the long Spanish connection as a risk to be approached with utmost caution. Her ambivalence drove her advisers to distraction, but she was torn: while being urged to fix her eyes on far horizons, she constantly felt pressure to turn them to nearby dangers and the possibility of disruptions at home.

The Crown was well advised to be watchful of signs of a domestic Catholic rising led by aristocratic families loyal to the old faith—some of them at the heart of the court—or by returning exiles from across the water. In church policy, Elizabeth attempted to walk a middle path: she accepted outward conformity without examination of individual conscience. Since many private reservations—and priest-holes—were secretly maintained, this very English solution was thoroughly acceptable.

Withdrawn by Henry VIII's divorce from union with the Holy Catholic and Apostolic Church of Rome, England—where the sovereign himself had initiated the break with papal alliance—had become the natural bulwark of growing religious minorities in the Catholic realms on the Continent. Martin Luther's protests of 1517 had incited the growth of German, Dutch, and Scandinavian movements for church reform, shortly paralleled in France and Switzerland by the teachings of John Calvin, and in Scotland by those of John Knox. Yet while Elizabeth could be a supportive and sometimes even a subsidizing sympathizer, intervening on behalf of Protestants in Catholic countries, she had always to remember the proven likelihood of Catholic foreign aid to the Irish at her back door; and the series of plots on her life unmasked by Sir Francis Walsingham's intelligence apparatus made evident the reality of Catholic forces restlessly biding their time at home.

Most of the conspiracies against Elizabeth anticipated her assassination and replacement on the English throne by her Scottish cousin, Mary Stuart. This Catholic former child-queen of France, in her widowhood queen of Scotland until forced by the scandals of her reign to abdicate to her infant son, had been given guarded refuge in England: there, she became an avidly active political-religious schemer. Yet it took years to bring Elizabeth to the point of signing Mary's death warrant—she shrank from the spectacle of royalty on the executioner's block—and even after signing the warrant, she denied having given permission for it to be carried out. Mary was executed on February 8, 1587.

And through the years, acute Spanish ambassadors to the English court served as intermediaries and accessories for England's Catholic plotters, and as intelligence sources for Spain's Catholic king.

Events in the Netherlands in the mid-1580s accelerated the reversal of English foreign policy toward Spain. The queen had supported the leadership of Dutch William the Silent, Protestant prince of Orange and head of the states-general; a fanatic Catholic assassin shot him at Delft in 1584. In 1585, Parma captured Antwerp. Since England could not risk leaving Parma's army in uncontested control less than a hundred miles from her own shores, Elizabeth concluded a treaty with the northern

Dutch that permitted her to place garrisons of her own troops at Flushing, on the delta of the River Schelde, and Brill, on the delta of the Rhine. These were the only deep-draft ports on the sand-barred Dutch coast—north of Brill, all the way to the Frisian Islands, the coast was a dike, a defiant NO ENTRY sign to the sea itself, on whose unbreached preservation the population behind it depended for their land, their livelihood, even their lives.

At the start of the campaigning season in the spring of 1586, Elizabeth sent over the earl of Leicester, in command of 5,000 infantry and 1,000 horse, and while his leadership proved both militarily faulty and politically abrasive, his presence forced Parma to defer an effort to conquer the coastal provinces of Zeeland and Holland. These remained in Dutch control, with indigenous seamen patrolling their coasts in their skillfully designed, shallow-draft flyboats and crampsters.

At various times, Spain had weighed the suitability of the Low Countries as a point of departure for an invasion of England. Don John of Austria, when he became regent of the Spanish holdings, had cherished a plan to cross the North Sea, free Mary Queen of Scots, marry her, and become another of Charles V's grandson-princes. In principle, Parma held conquest of England to be a necessary prelude to reliable control of the Netherlands, though he disagreed with Philip of Spain on the amount of preparation that the undertaking required, and unsuccessfully warned him against attempting the Enterprise of England in his state of readiness as of 1588.

Against the Spanish threat, England's defense had to come from her navy. The English had never had a standing army. Such experience of land fighting as existed had been obtained by the special levies raised for service in Ireland or on the Continent, or by free-lance troops recruited by private gentlemen for service under their own command. Creation and financing of an adequate fleet was therefore at the top of the long list of the monarchy's needs as foreign policy was reshaped with new objectives.

Elizabeth, like her father, selected most of her major government advisers, as contrasted with the officers of her court, from the gentry or below rather than from the aristocracy. Among others drawn from able but untitled stock were Sir William Cecil, the later Lord Burghley, her principal Private Secretary before he became her Lord Treasurer, and Sir Francis Walsingham, diplomat and intelligence chief. Both were Privy Councillors, and reduction of the Council to a workable size on her accession—attendance was usually under a dozen—heightened the policy-making effectiveness of its ministerial members. The counsels of the two men provided the regime with a remarkable balance. Burghley was the conservative, a shrewd, experienced, and cautious policy-maker opposed to much or rapid change and mindful of all its repercussions, domestic and foreign. With him as guide, the monarchy could be relied on to pursue a steady course. Walsingham was the advocate of innovation; he saw the vast opportunities for England in the new contest for world power, and was prepared to take risks lest they slip through Elizabeth's fingers. Her natural inclination was to follow Burghley's advice, but Walsingham's uncanny ear for successive plots against her life made her receptive to his proposals and the prospect of gold at the end of adventure. When her two advisers disagreed markedly, her choice might cause her foreign policy to zig and zag, but the two opposite forces usually vectored into long-term continuity.

With management of domestic government, Walsingham had little to do, but to Elizabeth and her Lord Treasurer, fulfillment of the old saying "The Prince must live of his own" caused persistent worry.

The Crown's income had to cover two public categories of expenditure: the cost of the display of state suitable to the court of a powerful sovereign, and the cost of operating the organs of government, from Parliament to the courts, from members of the Privy Council to the lowliest of customs collectors. In addition, there were the expenses of an absolute ruler's private pleasure. In Henry VIII's case, a fortunate overlap of private pleasure and public need led to his institution of a navy.

Henry had been the youth who disported himself in costume on the Thames blowing a boatswain's whistle; he was the Tudor monarch who commissioned the *Henri Grace à Dieu*, the splendid, high-charged, thousand-tonner more commonly known as the *Great Harry*, which in

Queen Elizabeth, with William Cecil, Lord Burghley, her Lord High
Treasurer, and Sir Francis Walsingham, her Secretary of State.

1520 had conveyed him in sumptuous display across the Channel to vie with the magnificence of France's François I at the Field of the Cloth of Gold; he became the navy-minded king who bequeathed a fleet of fifty-eight royal ships when he died. (Brilliant watercolors of these ships are still preserved in the Anthony Roll in the Pepysian Library at Magdalene College, Cambridge.) Elizabeth's half brother Edward and her half sister Mary did little for the navy that their father left them, but on her accession Elizabeth nevertheless inherited a roster of twenty-three vessels.

The new queen likewise inherited an administrative structure on which to build further strength. Henry had consistently maintained a Lord Admiral, and the noble Howard family, whose head was the duke of Norfolk, England's premier peer, enjoyed a near-monopoly of the post for a century and a half. In 1546, the king founded the Navy Board as an administrative agency to work under the Lord Admiral, managing naval affairs and supervising naval construction; he likewise set up three Trinity Houses, at Deptford, Kingston, and Newcastle, to see to the training of seamen.

For a good part of his reign, Henry's extravagant financial needs had been mitigated if not fully met by sales to private buyers of confiscated lands acquired by the Crown on his dissolution of the monastic houses. But he had gone through so much of this ecclesiastical windfall that he bequeathed a sizable debt to his successors, and Mary, in her turn, passed on some £200,000 of it, an amount equal to the Crown's annual income. So when Elizabeth began to build up her country's sea power, special devices had to be invented to pay for much of it.

Elizabeth's favor and Elizabeth's financial needs were closely intertwined. On the surface, her court was a place brilliant with Renaissance learning, with music of madrigal and lute and dancing of pavanes, with the pleasures of summer progresses and winter masques. Courtier poets allegorized and extolled in lovely lyrics the virtues and beauty of the red-haired Tudor princess of the delicate, long-fingered hands, Gloriana, their Virgin Queen. Thomas Dekker, in his *Pleasant Comedie of Old Fortunatus*, enumerates the guises under which the queen was addressed.

When asked "Are you then travelling to the temple of Eliza?" Old Fortunatus replies:

> Even to her temple are my feeble limbs travelling.
> Some call her Pandora: some Gloriana: some
> Cynthia: some Belphoebe: some Astraea; all by
> Several names to express several lives: Yet
> All those names make but one celestial body,
> As all those loves meet to create but one soul!
> I am of her own country, and we adore her by
> The name of Eliza.

But while the great courtier families trod the measures on her ceremonial occasions, they were also continually engaged in a competition, always fiercely jealous if usually smoothly low-key, for positions as well as position in her entourage. Gloriana normally enjoyed her contests with these inveterate importuners of royal benefice; in conducting them, she liked her courtiers to have style—a certain extravagance in dress, a certain suavity in manner, a certain capacity for repartee, a certain willingness to risk all in one reckless throw of the dice to catch her eye.

And while she dispensed much, the receiving was by no means all one way. The annual exchange of gifts at court on the anniversary of her accession in November and during the Christmas revels was profitable as well as pleasurable to her. John Nichols, in *Progresses and Public Processions of Queen Elizabeth*, published by him in 1823, footnotes his account of her visit to Sir Francis Walsingham in 1589 with this record of previous exchanges of gifts:

On New-year's day 1575–6, Mr. Secretary Walsingham presented to the Queen "a collar of gold, being two serpents, the heads being ophal a pyramid of sparks of dyamonds; in the top thereof a strawberry with a rock ruby; weight 5¾ ounces."—In 1577–8, Sir Francis presented "a gown of blue satin, with rows of gold; and two small perfume boxes, of Venice gold, faced with powdered armyns"; and Lady Walsingham gave "two pillow-biers of cambrick, wrought with silk of divers colours, cut." Sir Francis had, in return, 60½ ounces of gilt plate; his Lady 16¾ ounces. In the next year Sir Francis gave "a night-gown of tawny satin, all over embroidered, faced with satin like heare-colour"; and his Lady gave "a paire of gloves, with buttons of gold." In return, Sir Francis had three gilt bowls, weighing

59¾ ounces; his Lady 16½ ounces of gilt plate. In 1580–1 Lady Walsingham gave "a jewel of gold, being a scorpion of agatha, garnished with small sparks of rubies and diamonds."—Sir Francis and his Lady each presented New-year's Gifts to the Queen in 1588–9, and received each a present of plate in return.

On Elizabeth's summer progresses, her royal visits to noble houses temporarily relieved her of the expenses of her establishment as she honored the families who played host, often to the verge of bankruptcy. In 1591, for instance, at the invitation of the earl of Hertford, she stopped at Elventham House in Hampshire. As soon as she accepted, the earl, according to a contemporary description, "with all expedition set artificers to work":

First there was made a room of estate for the nobles, and at the end thereof, a withdrawing place for Her Majesty. The outsides of the walls were all covered with boughs, and clusters of ripe hazel nuts, the insides with arras, the roof of the place with works of ivy leaves, the floor with sweet herbs and green rushes.

Near adjoining unto this, were many offices newly builded, as namely spicery, lardery, chaundery, wine-cellar, ewery and pantry; all which were tiled. Not far off, was erected a large hall, for entertainment of knights, ladies and gentlemen of chief account. . . .

Between my Lord's house and the aforesaid hill, where these rooms were raised, there had been made in the bottom, by handy labour, a goodly pond, cut to the perfect figure of a half-moon. In this pond were three notable grounds, where hence to prevent [sic] Her Majesty with sports and pastimes. The first was a Ship Isle of 100 foot in length, and 40 foot broad, bearing three trees orderly set for three masts. The second was a Fort 20 foot square every way, and overgrown with willows. The third and last was a Snail Mount, rising in four spirals of green privy hedges, the whole in height 20 foot, and forty foot broad at the bottom. These three places were equally distant from the sides of the pond, and every one by a just measured proportion distant from other. In the said water were divers boats prepared for music, but especially there was a pinnace, full furnished with masts, yards, sails, anchors, cables and all other ordinary tackling; and with iron pieces, and lastly with flags, streamers and pendants, to the number of twelve, all painted with divers colours, and sundry devices. . . .

After supper there were two delights presented unto Her Majesty; curious fire-works, and a sumptuous banquet: the first from the three islands in the pond, the second in a low gallery in Her Majesty's privy garden. But I first will briefly speak of the fire-works.

The Great Pond at Elventham,
constructed for the earl of Hertford's entertainment of the queen in 1591.

First there was a peal of a hundred chambers discharged from the Snail Mount: in counter whereof, a like peal was discharged from the Ship Isle, and some great ordnance withal. Then was there a castle of fire-works of all sorts, which played in the Fort. Answerable to that, there was in the Snail Mount, a globe of all manner of fire-works, as big as a barrel. When these were spent on either side, there were many running rockets upon lines, which passed between the Snail Mount and the Castle in the Fort. On either side were many fire-wheels, pikes of pleasure, and balls of wild fire which burned in the water.

During the time of these fire-works in the water, there was a banquet served all in glass and silver, into the low gallery in the garden, from a hill-side fourteen score off, by two hundred of my Lord of Hertford's gentlemen, every one carrying so many dishes that the whole number amounted to a thousand, and there were to light them in their way a hundred torch-bearers.

Contributions of such brilliance not only gave pleasure to the queen; they were of material help in balancing the royal accounts. At the same time, in a very different area of finance, desire for military glory led gentlemen to spare the royal treasury by raising companies to go to Ireland and the Low Countries or Huguenot France. Best of all, the mercantile community in London and the chief towns was developing an invaluable economic mechanism, the joint-stock company, for financing ventures at sea. Such companies paid a considerable part in Elizabeth's creation of a powerful royal navy. The excitement of global discovery, like the excitement of space exploration four hundred years later, was in the air. Elizabeth was delighted to sanction the probing of newfound geographic areas by a means that both relieved her treasury and left her free to disavow the enterprise in case of determined foreign protest.

Ranking English merchants had long possessed private fleets for their Mediterranean and nearby coastal trade, and as overseas commerce increased, their financial chests had begun to approach and even rival those of such famous Continental houses as the Fuggers', from whom western European monarchs, including Elizabeth, had long negotiated massive loans. In the City of London, tales of returned explorers whetted appetites for both New World and Oriental voyages, and listening merchants offered loans and investments to further them.

When Elizabeth issued letters patent authorizing a venture, a private/public combination of support by aristocratic investors, well-to-do merchants, and the Crown could be put together. In addition to her grant of permission, she could usually be relied on to loan a ship—maybe two—or allow gunpowder to be drawn from royal stores, or advance a cash contribution that became a share in the profits. The private participants were expected to loan, lease, or buy other ships, pay suppliers, and hire crews, though when their efforts to sign on adequate numbers of seamen fell short, the queen was often willing to have her local justices of the peace use press gangs to round up necessary additions.

These expeditions were not expected to be solely exploratory. Captures on the high seas, sometimes justified as reprisals for previous wrongs but often indistinguishable from the piracies committed by professional freebooters, could pay the entire cost of an expedition; sales of the contents of a rich merchantman plus the value of the ship yielded goodly dividends to stockholders, money lenders, and the prize-taking crew. Established ratios governed the sharing of such gains: first, a fifth to the queen, plus 20 percent of any bullion or jewels on board, and a tenth as a perquisite to the Lord Admiral; then a division into thirds, one for the expedition's organizers and backers, prorated according to their input, one for the victuallers, and one for the crew. The crew's third was divided into "parts" and distributed according to rank: seven "parts" for the master, one apiece for the ship's boys, with the boatswain, the carpenter, the cook, and the common seamen in between. Many captured ships carried only everyday items—hides, salt, cloth—but a share in an exotic cargo could set a man up for life. Through such mercantile pursuits, England built up a generation of experienced captains, and a supply of seamen who "knew a rope."

They matured just in time. In 1578, the young king of Portugal was unexpectedly killed in a battle against the Moors. He left no immediately recognized heir, so during the next two years rival claimants bickered under the temporary government of an aged cleric. In 1580, Philip II ended the contest by an invasion that merged Portugal with Spain.

The advantages accruing to Philip—frontage on the Atlantic all the way from Cape Finisterre to Cape St. Vincent; such offshore islands as the Azores, the Canaries, and the Cape Verdes; the sea route to India, the Spice Islands, and Cathay—were more than England could tolerate in her new struggle for world power. Portuguese ships, guns, and experienced crews, now added to the Spanish fleet, speeded Philip's preparations for the Enterprise of England.

Five years later, Alessandro Farnese achieved the fall of Antwerp, and gave Philip a convenient base for an invasion of England. Farnese was the outstanding military leader of all Europe: he combined a capacity to plan far-reaching strategy, including close attention to the geographic peculiarities in which it would be carried out, with insistence on meticulous performance by the troops under his command.

Closeted in the Escorial, Philip became absorbed in preparing to convoy Parma's forces across the North Sea and defeat England's heretic queen. Secluded as a hermit, he issued orders and received written reports; he rarely saw the men who would lead his Enterprise of England, never visited the yards where his fleet was in the making, and did not even preside at Lisbon when his Invincible Armada, officially blessed in a ceremony at the cathedral, prepared to depart.

Perhaps he viewed the blessing as merely a formal confirmation of what had long been known: in his unshakeable belief, the policy of Spain, his policy, and the will of God were identical and inseparable. Did not images of Christ and Mary flank the royal arms on the banner under which the Armada sailed? Catholic reunion would follow his control of the country where a breach with Rome was maintained by its sovereign; it would accelerate the extinction of troublesome Protestant movements on the Continent. The universality of Christ's Holy and Apostolic Church would then be realized under a ruler known to be devoted body and soul to her interests—and at the same time the chief temporal competition to his enlarging empire would cease.

To meet this threat, Elizabeth had very little time. The quarter-century of English advance in the art of navigation and the design of fighting ships that came to fruition only months before it was tested was the work of an extraordinary generation of seafaring men.

Prior to that generation, English mariners had reached their destinations by following coasts or sailing from island to island. In addition to familiarity with winds and tides and the taking of soundings, navigation for such trips required little beyond use of compass cards whose lines showed the course to be held in order to reach a desired destination. But navigation on the high seas, with long periods out of sight of land, required different kinds of knowledge.

The new learning that spread with the Renaissance revolutionized the art of navigation. Gentlemen like Walter Ralegh, who gathered into their circles savants absorbed in geography, astronomy, and cosmology as intellectual pursuits, were aware of the application of these sciences to seafaring. They sped the development and use of new apparatus and the

Philip II, king of Spain (reigned 1556–98).

A gathering of savants and sailors to exchange navigational knowledge.

preparation of mathematical tables in forms accessible to mariners. New maps were continually appearing. Simplified manuals, "regiments for the sea," began to be published, describing how to make and how to use cross-staff and astrolabe for calculating latitude (except during eclipses of the moon, longitude was not accurately measured until the eighteenth century), how to estimate a ship's run and maintain a traverse board, how to keep a log.

A new breed of mariners multiplied, adept in navigation by sun and star. Their experience led to new shapes and sizes for ships, new plans for arming them, new strategies for fighting that armament in naval combat. Published in 1584, Robert Norman's poem "The Safeguard of Sailors" mentions some of the equipment of their ocean-crossing art:

> Whoso in surging Seas, his season will consume,
> And means thereof to make his onely trade to live
> That man must surely know the shifting Sunne & Moone,
> For trying of his Tides, how they doe take and give.
>
> Thus when he all the night, with wearie toyle hath tride,
> And sees the swelling seas hath set him from his waye:
> Then when a little slacke of calme he hath espide,
> With joyfull heart to take the height he doth assay.
>
> His *Astrolabe* then he setteth for the Sunne,
> Or *Cross-staffe* for the starre called *Ballastile*:
> And thus with help of them and declination,
> How land doth beare of him, he knowes within a while.
>
> Then by his *Compasse* straight he duly sets his course,
> And thus he brings the ship in safetie to her Porte,
> Where of his hazards past he makes a great discourse,
> And each man (by desert) doth give him good reporte.

With the exception of Martin Frobisher, the Yorkshireman who caught Humphrey Gilbert's eye as a promising lad, was his companion thereafter, and died in Plymouth, all of the greatest of these new captains were Devonians, born on the English peninsula that thrusts furthest into the Western Ocean. And by a curious coincidence, all were part of a vast and varied cousinry that by blood or marriage linked the Hawkinses, Humphrey Gilbert, John Davis, Richard Grenville, Francis Drake, and Walter Ralegh. With their knowledge, skill, and temper, these seasoned seamen held England's future in their keeping when the largest sailing fleet that ever put to sea appeared at the entrance to the English Channel.

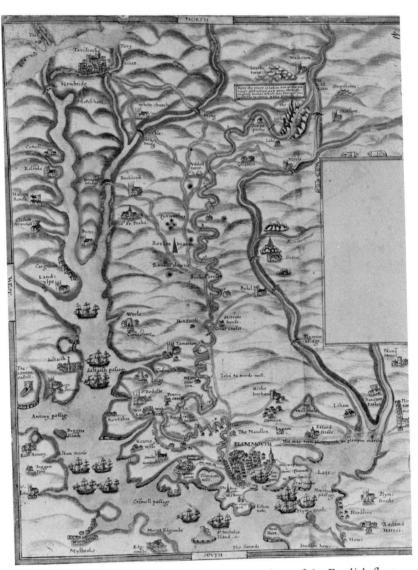

Plymouth Harbor, where the western squadron of the English fleet
awaited the arrival of the Armada of 1588.

II

The Mercantile Hawkinses

EVONSHIRE IS SHAPED FOR THE SEA; BETWEEN the high furzy wastes of Exmoor in the north and Dartmoor in the south, profitable only to tough-toothed sheep, long rivers flow past fertile fields to estuaries that pour their waters into the Atlantic or the English Channel. In the north, Bideford at the mouth of the Torridge and Barnstaple at the mouth of the Taw share their Atlantic exit; at the cathedral city of Exeter the Exe broadens its southbound flow to Exmouth; at Plymouth, the Plym on the east of the city and the Tavy and the Tamar on the west converge to form the most extensive harbor on the southwest Devon coast.

It was to Plymouth, when the great age of sixteenth-century exploration started, that John Hawkins, a landsman from Tavistock on the Tavy, with his bride, Joan Amadas of Launceston, moved to set up a marine merchandising business. Soon Hawkins's warehouses began to rise alongside the wharves of Plymouth's inner harbor, given night-time security by the heavy iron chain stretched across the narrow entrance at the barbican. Initially, they received cargoes brought by sea captains of Hawkins-owned ships returning from coastal voyages. Some of the ships would have crossed the Channel, sailed around the Breton peninusula, and passed between the grim-walled bastions guarding La Rochelle's inner harbor to trade there, or threaded their way up the estuary of the Gironde to load cargoes of French wines at the long curve of the Bordeaux waterfront. Others would have crossed the often malignant Bay of Biscay to fetch hogsheads of port from Oporto in Portugal or visit the harbor of Cadiz to pick up consignments from English factors resident in Sanlúcar and Seville—these usually included some of the wine from Jerez that was called sherry when it reached home port. Occasionally, skippers even passed the Pillars of Hercules into the Mediterranean, in spite of the ever-active risk of meeting the Barbary Coast pirates off Morocco.

After ships began to be built at Hawkins-owned yards in Plymouth, the Hawkinses themselves sometimes became seafarers and captained their vessels over still longer courses. John Hawkins's son William, the first of three generations to bear the name, began the tradition: in the latter 1520s this William sailed his *Paul of Plymouth* to trading points in Africa along the Guinea coast, and more than once crossed the ocean to Brazil and the New World. A ballad of the next century, "The Jovial Mariner," lauds the spirit of these voyages:

> I am a Jovial Mariner, our calling is well known,
>   We trade with many a Foreigner, to purchase high renown;
> We serve our country faithfully, and bring home store of gold;
> We do our business manfully, for we are free and bold:
>   *A Sea-man hath a valiant heart, and bears a noble minde,*
>   *He scorneth once to shrink or start for any stormy wind.*
>
> Brave *England* hath been much inricht by art of Navigation;
>   Great store of wealth we home have fetched for to adorn our Nation:
> Our Merchants still we do supply with Traffick that is rare,
> Then Sea-men cast your caps on high, we are without compare.
>   *A Sea-man hath a valiant heart, and bears a noble minde,*
>   *He scorneth once to shrink or start for any stormy wind.*

During the course of a navy stint as master of the *Great Galley*, the first William Hawkins made an acquaintance of later importance to his family when he came to know a Bristol seaman, Captain William Gonson, Henry VIII's Paymaster of the Fleet whom the king named Clerk of the Ships when he created the office in 1524.

By the 1530s, William Hawkins I had accumulated the eminence and affluence to warrant entry into Plymouth politics. He was elected mayor, first in 1532–33, again in 1538–39. He was Plymouth's parliamentary representative, both in 1539, when King Henry's dissolution of the monasteries was completed, and in 1547, the year the child-king Edward VI came to the throne.

The Hawkins firm also served the Protestant cause by privateering in the Channel: before the French attempt to invade England in 1545, William I and his associates, having obtained letters of marque, were busy harassing French shipping with a fleet of up to ten barks; the letters stipulated that they must cover their own costs, but gave them the right to impress crews and obtain victuals and arms.

William I's last Parliament was in 1553, the year before his death. His son William II then stepped into his father's shoes as a foremost citizen. He had served as mayor twice before his election in 1587–88, when he took charge of the borough's preparations for the Armada.

Under him, the firm's outreach overseas was extended: the regular ports of call of his merchantmen included the Canary Islands, the last stop where English transatlantic fleets could water on their outbound journeys. With the exception of one West Indies passage of which little is known, William himself rarely went to sea; the anchor of the family firm, he stayed home among the ledger books and kept the store.

In the early 1570s, when Sir Richard Grenville and other West Country gentlemen requested letters patent from the queen for a voyage that should include colonization as well as exploration in the New World, William offered to become an investor; but shortly after Her Majesty gave permission for the voyage, she rescinded it. He sent the sizable *Castle of Comfort*, of which he was part owner, and other vessels to support the revolt of the Protestant Low Countries against their Spanish occupiers, and the Protestant French in their struggle against the Catholic League. And when a Spanish ship loaded with the wages of Spanish troops was forced to seek harbor at Plymouth, he was happy to act with Sir Arthur Champernoune, Lord Lieutenant of Devon, in holding her as a prize until the queen should decide whether the money had to be returned to the Spanish authorities. (She decided against it.) Both the French and the Spanish king repeatedly protested his activities.

Within his immediate family, William II saw to the upbringing of the dynasty's third William. When about seventeen, in 1577, this lad shipped with Drake on his round-the-world voyage, the first by an Englishman. In 1582, William III sailed under the command of Edward Fenton on what Richard Hakluyt, in his maritime records, referred to as the "troublesome" voyage. (The Fenton expedition was planned as an overt challenge to Spain: Philip II, after absorbing Portugal, had assumed the right to the route to the Far East around the Cape of Good Hope that the Portuguese had pioneered, and the English had determined to use it themselves. But Fenton's top command was fissured by a quarrel over whether the fleet should actually go by way of the Cape of Good Hope, as they had been directed to do, or through the Strait of Magellan around South America as some of those on board had recently done. In the end, the expedition abandoned its mission and came home, having traveled no further than to Brazil.) In the Armada year, William III commanded the *Griffin*, sailing with the western squadron of the fleet out of Plymouth.

About the time that William III was born, his uncle John Hawkins, thirteen years younger than William III's father, was engaged in a series of voyages that in their later importance far outdistanced the other exploits of the family firm. Like the rest of the family, John had been brought up as part of the Plymouth establishment, learning much about the sea at first hand, listening to the tales of his grandfather, his father, his brother, and the captains in their employ, and on shore absorbing much of the careful accounting procedures that make a merchant successful. Then, in his early thirties, he undertook the first of three transatlantic expeditions, sailing from Plymouth but funded from London.

Spain forbade foreigners from trading with its settlements in the West Indies and around the Caribbean and the Gulf of Mexico, but such extensive coasts could not be effectively monitored. In many places, surreptitious markets throve as a result of the demand for desired consumer commodities, and especially for Negro slaves, who were bought and sold like other goods. To serve this demand, Hawkins took charge of three ships—the 120-ton *Saloman*, the 100-ton *Swallow*, the 40-ton *Jonas*—and with about a hundred men sailed to Africa in October 1562, procured some 300 Negroes at Sierra Leone, and crossed to Hispaniola. He sold the slaves, bought hides, ginger, sugar, and pearls with the proceeds, and returned without incident.

In October 1564 he sailed again, with the addition of the 700-ton

The *Jesus of Lübeck*,
purchased from Hanseatic merchants for the royal fleet by Henry VIII and
sailed to the Caribbean by John Hawkins in the 1560s.

Jesus of Lübeck, loaned by the queen, and further backing from the earls of
Pembroke and Leicester. The huge *Jesus* afforded carrying capacity for
many more slaves, but this time, Hawkins had to join a war of one tribe
against another in order to procure some, and on arrival in the Indies he
had difficulty obtaining local licenses to sell and buyers to buy at prices
he thought proper. Before starting home, he stopped in Florida, where
he offered relief to a Huguenot colony on the peninsula and raided the
Spanish fort at St. Augustine. He then coasted north to pick up cod in
Newfoundland, and reached Cornwall in late September 1565. (Years
later, when Hawkins became a member of the Navy Board, the coat of
arms granted to him bore a crest of "a demi-Moor properly coloured,
bound by a cord," in remembrance of these slaving voyages.)

The third voyage, begun in 1567, ended in humiliating defeat, and burned an abiding hate of everything Spanish into the memory of both Hawkins and young Francis Drake, who captained a small boat in his company. By this time, Spain had formally protested John Hawkins's presence in its territories to Elizabeth, and sent instructions to all island and mainland governors to be on the lookout and prevent trade if he reappeared. In riposte, the queen loaned him another of her large ships, the *Minion*, in addition to the *Jesus*. The Hawkins firm sent its own *William and John* and the smaller *Swallow*, *Angel*, and *Judith*.

Because of various delays, Hawkins was still in the Caribbean at the beginning of the hurricane season in late summer 1568. A storm of the violence usual at that time of year seriously damaged the old high-castled *Jesus*—she dated from Henry VIII's time—and the shoals around Florida offered no harbor to take in a ship of her draft for repairs. Hawkins was considering abandoning her when a second storm hit his fleet, battering enough of the ships to decide him to seek admission for repair and water at San Juan de Ulua, the Spanish settlement on the east coast of the Gulf of Mexico that served as port for the headquarters of the governor-general.

He arrived at an awkward moment. Spanish ships already there were loaded with gold and silver, momentarily awaiting the convoy that would shepherd them to Seville. The convoying ships—thirteen of them—hove in sight the very next day, and they carried New Spain's new governor. Sensing trouble, Hawkins proposed arrangements to keep the peace in the harbor, and the Spanish agreed to them.

They did not keep the agreement. As Hawkins fought his way out, his heavily outnumbered ships were incapacitated, one after another. He used the *Jesus* for its final service as a shelter behind which he collected in the *Minion* men who swam their way from other ships or out from shore as the guns barked overhead, and transshipped some of the stores the *Jesus* had carried. When the fight was over, only the *Minion* was able to sail; Hawkins's other seaworthy craft, the little 50-ton *Judith*, commanded by Drake, had departed for England without further word. The *Minion*, very empty of victuals and very full of men, had to start a transatlantic passage with much of the stormy season still ahead. When some of the men, realizing that if they stayed aboard they would be driven to "eate hides, cats, rats, parrots, munkies and doggies," asked to be set ashore, Hawkins let them off.

(It was twenty-three years before Job Hortop, a sailor who had swum out to the *Minion* and then had chosen to disembark, reached England again; he set down his account of meeting with savages, enslavement in Mexico, transfer to Spain, long imprisonment, and punishment. Eventually, Robert Barrett, his ship's master and Drake's cousin, was burned at the stake, and Hortop and others were condemned to row in Spain's galleys. After an exceptional twelve-year record of survival at the oars, he was returned to life imprisonment, but by promising seven years of private servitude to an official, he contrived his release, and shortly escaped to a French ship that to his great good luck was then captured by an Englishman.)

In the *Minion*, Hawkins limped home, stopping for relief in Galicia before arriving in late January 1569 at Mount's Bay in Cornwall. Shortly after he was back, he and Lord Burghley connived in a piece of diplomatic double-dealing that brought him a certain measure of solace for his defeat. Hawkins deceived the Spanish king with an offer of his services. Believing him, Philip freed some of the prisoners and hostages Hawkins had yielded and sent the Englishman £40,000 and a title as a Spanish grandee. Hawkins's new status enabled him to secure evidence of the plot in which Philip's emissaries in England were conspiring with the duke of Norfolk to supplant Elizabeth with Mary Queen of Scots on the English throne; he thereby established useful credit with the queen's chief adviser.

Soon after his return, Hawkins terminated his membership in the family firm at Plymouth and extended the range of the Hawkins dynasty by moving to London. Here, he could witness the full strength of the merchant interest in ventures to distant sources of greatly desired goods.

Though eventually the most prominent, Plymouth was by no means the only port to support a sixteenth-century marine dynasty. In Chichester, on the south-central coast, the Fenner family produced three of the captains of major ships in the western squadron against the Armada; and when John Hawkins reached London, he met a rival from the ranking maritime family of Bristol.

At the end of the previous century, after the Venetian navigator John Cabot came to England with his three sons, offering his services to Henry VIII, and settled in Bristol, the merchants there backed his voyages along the northern North American coast—to Greenland, Newfoundland, Labrador—and south past Cape Cod as far as the shores of Chesapeake Bay. The Bristol seaman John Winter, who had served in Henry VIII's navy, became the progenitor of a dynasty that rivaled the Hawkinses, and in the reign of Edward VI, Cabot's son Sebastian, after many years of service to Spain, returned to London to be appointed England's Chief Pilot and become governor of the Merchant Adventurers Company.

These were the years when Sir Thomas Gresham walked the streets of London's financial district as the leading figure among English banker-princes. From 1551 to 1574, he operated as the English Crown's factor in Antwerp, as his father had done before him, negotiating loans, overseeing repayments, and procuring Continental specialties such as the heavy brass cannon now being mounted below decks on fighting ships. When, in the latter 1560s, he ordered built in London an ornate edifice, rivaling in style the comparable building erected in Antwerp thirty-five years earlier, it was for the convenience of London bankers and merchants dealing in overseas currencies who previously had conducted their transactions in a twice-daily hubbub amid other desecrations going on in the nave of St. Paul's. In a candlelight visit to its arcaded courtyard one evening in 1571, after dining at Sir Thomas's mansion in Bishopsgate, Queen Elizabeth inspected the shops in its cloisters and bestowed on it the name of the Royal Exchange. Today's replacement, built on the site after a nineteenth-century fire, continues to be topped by Gresham's personal emblem, the grasshopper on his family crest.

At the time of his death, Sir Thomas was reckoned the wealthiest commoner in England. His daily associates, complementing the bankers who dealt in currencies, were the merchants who, though they frequently made loans, dealt primarily in goods. These were the men most apt to participate as shareholders and even as furnishers of ships for exploratory voyages, anticipating their return either with prizes taken at sea or salable commodities purchased in distant ports. Among them was William Sanderson, whose Yorkshire grandfather had moved to London at the end of the fifteenth century and whose father, also a William Sanderson, had engaged in merchandising as an active trader until his death in 1570 at the ripe old age of eighty-six. The third William, of the prime Elizabethan period, was both a trader and a widely traveled man of broad interests, fascinated by the current spread of geographical knowledge and its transmission through revised maps. The pair of globes he ordered from the city's ranking craftsman, Emery Molyneux, as a gift to the queen, can be seen in the Greenwich Museum today. There are several cartouches on the globes, and beside one of them, in Latin and English, are lines in which Sanderson addresses the public:

> Not in the lappe of learned skill, I ever was upbrought
> Nor in the study of the starres (wth griefe I graunt) was taught
> Yet whilst on this side arts, on that syde vertues honor
> My minde admiring viewd, and rested fixt upon her
> Loo at my charge then seest ye ever whirling Sphere
> The endles reaches of the land, and sea in sight appeare
> For cōntries good, for worlds behoofe, for learnings fourtherance
> Wherby our vertios englishmen their actions may advāce
> To visite forraine landes, where farthest coastes do lye
> I have these worldes thus formd, and to worldes good apply
> Wth word I pray you favor them [& furt]her them with will
> That arts and vertue may be deckt, wth their due honor still
> But yf that any better have, let them the better shewe
> For lernings sake, I will not spare ye charges to bestowe.

This Sanderson's weakness for investment in the voyages of the great Devonians may have been due in part to the influence of his Cornish wife,

Mary Snedale; she was the child of Ralegh's stepsister, and of their seven sons the first three were named Ralegh, Cavendish, and Drake. Sanderson was said to have backed Sir Walter's expenditures for his Virginia voyages and other ventures to a total of £100,000, and financed his private debt for as much as £16,000 at a time; he was comparably interested in John Davis's searches for a Northwest Passage, and later in the century in various probes of the Far East.

Like the Devon captains, most merchants were from the rising gentry. While trade had traditionally been frowned on as a springboard for social advancement, at the rate at which the wealth and economic power of London was advancing its prime movers could hardly be permanently snubbed by an aristocracy hitherto based on hereditary holdings of land. The wealth of the new stock companies that took shape in the sixteenth and early seventeenth centuries—the Merchant Adventurers Company and the Muscovy, the Levant, and the East India companies—was burgeoning in a city whose life had long been dominated by the great liveried companies serving domestic needs, of which there were some two dozen in all, including apothecaries, armorers, goldsmiths, mercers, and vintners. And like the Hawkinses of Plymouth, members of the growing merchant class became sheriffs, aldermen, and lords mayor in the nation's capital. Of the ninety-seven lords mayor who served between 1509 and 1603, seventy-two had made their money in the cloth trade. Such power could not be indefinitely ignored.

The specific reason for John Hawkins's move to London stemmed from the chance relationship of William Hawkins I with William Gonson, Henry VIII's Paymaster of the Fleet: in 1569, John married Katherine, Gonson's granddaughter. Her father, Benjamin, was now the Navy Board's treasurer. Hawkins spent a few years serving as his father-in-law's assistant and representing Plymouth in Parliament. Then, on Benjamin's retirement in 1577, Hawkins succeeded him as treasurer. In this post, over the decade 1578–88, he revolutionized the shape of English ships and supervised the building and rebuilding program that gave Elizabeth a fleet strong enough to meet Philip's Armada.

Benjamin Gonson had been accurate when, on retiring, he remarked to his son-in-law, "I shall pluck out a thorn from my foot, and put it in yours." All too soon, Hawkins met serious resistance from other members of the Board as he introduced new administrative arrangements. He had joined a bureaucracy well equipped for governmental infighting, and more than ready to exercise its competence on the newcomer to its ranks.

The Board was riddled with nepotism. Hawkins's own appointment had followed prevalent procedure: William Gonson had served as navy paymaster for twenty years from 1524 until his death in 1544. John Winter of Bristol replaced him, but died within the year. When the Navy Board was founded, in 1546, the office of paymaster became that of treasurer, and Benjamin Gonson inherited it. So it seemed suitable for Hawkins to take over the office of his father-in-law on the latter's retirement. But once installed, he did not play by the rules.

Hawkins especially irked the Board member who was a successor of John Winter, his son William who became the Board's Surveyor of the Ships in 1549, and in 1557 acquired a second office, Master of Ordnance; the two posts together gave him control of armament and victualling.

William's brother George became Clerk of the Ships about 1560 and held the office for over twenty years until he died.

William Holstocke, who had served Henry VIII, became the Board's Controller in 1562, and held the post for twenty-seven years until his death in 1589.

As comfortable cronies, these men, while acquiring their formidable seniority, had placed numerous kinsmen and adherents in subordinate positions. They were accustomed to a leisurely pace of work, and to overseeing a navy that operated almost entirely in the Channel and the North Sea. Such was the solid block of civil-service structure that Hawkins had to move.

In Tudor times, the pursuit of perquisites was customary. Elizabeth's frugal policy of paying only nominal salaries to her officials encouraged many—indeed, most—to augment their basic stipends by exploiting opportunities that opened up in the performance of their duties. The

Sir William Winter, member of the Navy Board, Master
of Ordnance and Surveyor of the Ships in the years
before the Armada of 1588.

practice was so general as to be more or less taken for granted, and construction and repair of ships offered endless possibilities. Lord Burghley himself, who received only £400 a year as Lord High Treasurer, was heard to complain that "my fees of my treasureship do not answer my charge of my stable—I mean not my *table!*" He depended rather on the patronage offered by this office, plus his more lucrative appointment as Master of the Wards.

Since Hawkins had been working under Gonson for some time before he replaced him, he came into office with a fair idea of what had been going on at the Board at the expense of the Crown. Very shortly, his training at the Plymouth family firm had enabled him to put together some hard figures. With these in hand, he went to the Lord Treasurer. He reminded Burghley that, under existing procedure, the Navy Board voted as a whole, and consequently could overrule its treasurer and authorize outpayments beyond what he proposed. Illustrating current abuses, he stated that two of William Winter's ships, the *Edward* and the *Mary Fortune*, had been built from Elizabeth's timber. The timber for the *Foresight*, the first ship of a new naval type, had been paid for twice. When an old ship was broken up, the metal fittings were not re-used on the successor. And so on. Burghley, who had sniffed corruption at the Board as early as 1571, listened willingly as Hawkins, a man of order with a merchant's attention to input and outgo, and increasingly a Puritan, proposed strict alternative procedures for handling the Board's funds.

Hawkins successfully suggested that the queen should place a ceiling of £2,200 on ordinary expenses for the navy, authorizing two contracts, one to be made with him, for £1,200, and one with her two master shipwrights, Peter Pett and Matthew Baker, for £1,000. The shipwrights' contract would cover regular operating costs at the various yards: on a five-year schedule, they would ground all ships of the fleet at regular intervals, renewing the weaker strakes below the water line; every year, they would ransack (empty of ballast and clean) all ships, and caulk and repair them above the water line. They would keep ships' boats in shape and equip outgoing vessels for emergency repairs at sea.

ÆTATIS SVÆ LVIII
Ano Dni 1591

Sir John Hawkins.

Though they could draw on the naval stores at Chatham for trees for the lower sections of masts and for yards on the large ships, they would themselves supply masts and yards for vessels below 200 tons. And they would pay for the wages, keep, and tools of the men who worked under them.

Hawkins's contract would buy the canvas, cables, hawsers, ropes, and lines used to anchor and operate the fleet—the most quickly expended of ship's gear, the proper care of which could yield substantial savings.

Extraordinary expenses, such as dry-docking or the building of new ships, would be met by special authorizations under present rules.

The two contracts, known as the "first bargain," ran from 1579 to 1584. Hawkins had estimated that their acceptance would save the queen about £4,000 annually, and he was able to prove his point. He had told Burghley that in the mid-'70s annual expenditures had averaged almost £6,000 (actually £5,822) when £4,000 would have sufficed for the items covered by the bargain; in the books Hawkins kept during the first bargain, they came to £3,908.

The "second bargain," made in 1585, was a single contract for £4,000, with Hawkins in sole control; it covered not only the items formerly listed as ordinary but also the cost for staff of the harbor service and the garrison at Upnor Castle that guarded warships moored in the Medway, and repair of wharves and storehouses at Portsmouth, Deptford, Woolwich, and Chatham. Another £1,714.2.2 was provided for extraordinary items, materials for heavy repairs, and wages of workers doing the repairs. With this total, Hawkins remade the English fleet.

The arming of the ships, Sir William Winter's province, had always been a separate operation: the Ordnance Office was in the Tower, where munitions for both army and navy—guns of all sizes, powder, and shot—were stored. Food and drink were likewise obtained separately through Winter's other office as General Surveyor of Victuals for the Sea. (Victualling presented an almost insoluble problem: if a ship were stocked much ahead of time, food became putrid and drink seeped out of its casks; yet if deferred to the last moment, the assembly of enough supplies to keep an entire fleet at sea for a long period was difficult to impossible.)

To the cronies on the Board, Hawkins's allegations regarding previous practices were thoroughly reprehensible. He was a Johnny-come-lately, a troublemaker, and unlike themselves, a provincial to boot. They were true Londoners (Winter had forgotten about Bristol), while Hawkins had come to town only after his marriage. Hawkins's portrait by the Antwerp master Hieronimo Custodis, now at Buckland Abbey, shows a meticulously dressed gentleman, hardly a country bumpkin. (In 1573 he had been stabbed while driving down the Strand by an assailant who mistook him for Elizabeth's notably dandified vice-chamberlain.) But to the Board, he was an outport man.

Led by Winter, the infighting began at once. Hawkins, foreseeing it, had spiked some of Winter's guns by calling attention to the fact that since boatswains, gunners, and pursers owed their jobs to Winter, they could hardly be expected to give unbiased testimony regarding the Board's past delinquencies. As witnesses in his favor, Hawkins thought that pride in craftsmanship might lend independence to the queen's two master shipwrights, Peter Pett and Matthew Baker. Pett—he was the third generation of the royal family of naval designers and builders, and three more generations were to follow him—backed Hawkins. The crotchety Matthew Baker was less friendly, but he and Hawkins shared a fervent belief that high-castled ships were inferior to those of lower profile; whenever one of the large old ships came in for repair, between the two of them the repair was likely to become a rebuilding. A manuscript book to which Baker was a large contributor still exists in the Pepysian Library at Magdalene College, Cambridge; in it is one of Baker's drawings of an uncastled hull with the shape of a fish superimposed upon it—Baker said that the more a ship resembled a fish, the likelier it was to rival the performance of a fish in the water.

(While Pett and Baker intervened rather even-handedly in the infighting on the Navy Board, they gave way to their own jealousies when a new man was named master shipwright and injected himself into their own coziness. Richard Chapman of Deptford became the third master in

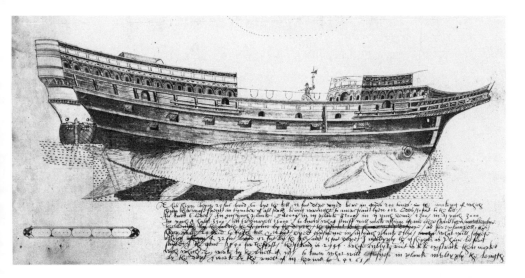

Master Shipwright Matthew Baker's drawing of a hulk with a fish
superimposed. Baker believed that a ship could perform most successfully
if its shape resembled that of a fish.

Ship-designer and aide.

1587. They could not deny his competence; he had just completed the new-style *Tramontana* and his next job was Sir Walter Ralegh's *Ark*; yet they resented his arrival—even though his wife was Pett's sister Anne.)

However, in the conflict of testimony, the Board's old members also mustered weighty support. Among the more telling depositions against Hawkins was that of a servant of Lord Leicester who had observed operations at the yards when his master's galleon, the *Leicester*, was in for repairs. After acknowledging Hawkins's graciousness, he lists the charges they talked over:

. . . say what I would, or object what I would, he would seem to make such sound answer or avoidance of the matter, and would with such a grace and face maintain his matter, that he made me sometimes think that I had mistaken that which now I know I perfectly know. . . .

Amongst many other matters that were between us talked upon, as the boutchinge [botching] of the ships and deceiving the Queen in his professed savings; the general clamours of numbers of people against him whose living they said he and his wife did take away; the parts of ships' adventures and purchases which he had and made; the abuses committed in the storehouse by him and some others by buying cordage and canvas at one price, and thrusting it into the storehouse by turns at higher prices; the taking of timber by commission and employing it to his own private buildings and profits by selling it, converting it into sugar chests, or repairing his own and other men's ships. . . .

The list was long.

Charge and countercharge reached a level at which an investigatory commission had to be appointed. Its members were Privy Councillors— the Lord Treasurer, the Lord High Admiral, the Lord Chamberlain, Sir Francis Walsingham, and his brother-in-law Sir Walter Mildmay, the Lord Chancellor. Using their power to appoint sub-commissioners, they added such navigators as Drake, Frobisher, and the Ralegh brothers. Later, this commission became the source of policy for national defense.

No record of its findings on graft in the shipyards has survived, but it is obvious that Hawkins came out pretty well. Over the next years, secure in his "bargains," he pushed production at the yards at a truly remarkable rate. Every day, the air was lively with the nick of adzes on timber, the high-pitched ring of hammers on spikes, the low-pitched

Shipyard worker climbing up to set a "knee" on the frame of a vessel under construction.

thunk of sledges on glowing metal at the forge, and the shouts of foremen as gangs upended heavy masts to drop them through the deck-holes of new ships to their seatings on the keels—with the smell of hot pitch over everything.

Ship by ship, the speed of new construction can be documented, for a list of the royal fleet in the year of the Armada shows the dates at which each ship was worked on. The three largest of the high old-fashioned vessels still remaining in the navy—the 1,100-ton *Triumph*, the 1,000-ton *Bear*, and the 900-ton *Elizabeth Jonas*—all dating from 1559–64, took part against the Armada without substantial alteration; their size and height matched that of the Spanish galleons. The next largest, Hawkins's own command when the Spanish came, the 800-ton *Victory*, had been built in 1560 but was rebuilt in 1586. The 500-ton *Revenge* came off the ways in the year of transfer of responsibility from Gonson to Hawkins; she was Drake's flagship when he served as Vice Admiral of the Fleet against the Armada. What particularly distinguishes the *Revenge* was that she was the prototype of the fighting ship of the future—smaller, faster, more maneuverable, handled as a gun-carriage in the new science of naval strategy. Her rating of 500 tons was duplicated in most of the others in the new class—none was over 800 tons. Hawkins merely gave her a thorough overhaul, but he either rebuilt or built, from the keel up, her seven sisters. They were his first concern: by the end of 1584 he had rebuilt four of them, the *Nonpareil*, the *Lion*, the *Hope*, and the *Elizabeth Bonadventure*. In 1586–87, in the nick of time, he completed three all-new ones, including the Lord High Admiral's flagship; they were the *Vanguard*, the *Rainbow*, and the *Ark Royal*.

Of the thirteen ships of from 400 tons downward, the *Foresight*, the *Swiftsure*, the *Dreadnought*, and the *Achates* dated from before Hawkins's time; during it, the *Bull* and the *Tiger* were rebuilt; the rest were new. Of the seven new pinnaces, one was finished in '83 and one in '85; five were begun and launched in the single year 1586.

Once this breathtaking output was at sea and began to be tested, actual experience and rising patriotism combined to end the bickering at the Navy Board. The old Board members' favorite dismissal of Hawkins's low costs as being due to Hawkins's lowering of quality in materials and workmanship began to sound a little hollow as shake-down cruises proved the opposite. Old scores were forgotten; even Winter reversed himself to join the chorus of praise for the fleet's fitness: "Our ships do show themselves like gallants here. I assure you it will do a man's heart good to behold them; and would to God the Prince of Parma were upon the seas with all his forces, and we in view of them."

The Lord High Admiral's letters to Burghley marvel at the ships' condition. On February 21, 1588, he declared: "I have been aboard of every ship that goeth out with me, and in every place where any may creep, and I do thank God that they be in the estate that they be in, and there is never a one of them that knows what a leak means."

Eight days later, he wrote again: "I protest before God, and as my soul shall answer for it, that I think there were never in any place of the world worthier ships than these are, for so many. And as few as we are, if the King of Spain's forces be not hundreds, we will make good sport with them."

The next month, he reported a specific incident: "The *Elizabeth Bonadventure*, in coming in, by the fault of the pilot came aground on a sand. . . . The next tide, by the goodness of God and great labour, we brought her off, and in all this time there never came a spoonful of water into her well. My Lord, except a ship had been made of iron, it were to be thought to be unpossible to do as she hath done."

During the running of the Armada, none of the fleet that Hawkins had readied developed faults. Without his driving force—and constant scrutiny—such a result would have been, as Lord Howard said, "unpossible."

Yet in the midst of the pressure, Hawkins enjoyed one respite, if an active command could be given that name. It had long been the custom for Navy Board members to serve at sea from time to time, and in late 1586 he was happy, with William Borough as his vice admiral, to lead five of the queen's ships, the *Nonpareil*, *Lion*, *Hope*, *Revenge*, and *Tramontana*, together with various merchantmen and pinnaces, down the Channel to patrol the Spanish coast and the route between Spain and the

Azores. Both he and Drake were warm advocates of the view that the best defense was an offense, but in this case his attempted sweep of Spanish shipping—his start delayed by rumors of a possible French strike at England from Brittany—missed its mark: both the year's home-coming fleet from the West Indies and the carracks from East India reached Spanish ports without interception.

When commands were assigned for the Armada, the Navy Board was skeletonized; now was the moment to leave administration and display fighting skill. Hawkins, Winter, and William Borough, who since early in the decade had been Clerk of the Ships, all departed; only William Holstocke was left behind.

After the Armada had disappeared into the northern mists, Hawkins summarized to Walsingham the ten days in which the queen's ships were tested. The terseness of his letter revives the action, and its close foresees the difficulties of the days that followed the fleet's return:

My bounden duty humbly remembered unto your good lordship:—I have not busied myself to write often to your lordship in this great cause, for that my lord Admiral doth continually advertise the manner of all things that doth pass. So do others that understand the state of all things as well as myself. We met with this fleet somewhat to the westward of Plymouth upon Sunday in the morning, being the 21st of July, where we had some small fight with them in the afternoon. By the coming aboard one of the other of the Spaniards, a great ship, a Biscayan, spent her foremast and bowsprit; which was left by the fleet in the sea, and so taken up by Sir Francis Drake the next morning. The same Sunday there was, by a fire chancing by a barrel of powder, a great Biscayan spoiled and abandoned, which my lord took up and sent away.

The Tuesday following, athwart of Portland, we had a sharp and long fight with them, wherein we spent a great part of our powder and shot, so as it was not thought good to deal with them any more till that was relieved.

The Thursday following, by the occasion of the scattering of one of the great ships from the fleet, which we hoped to have cut off, there grew a hot fray, wherein some store of powder was spent; and after that, little done till we came near to Calais, where the fleet of Spain anchored, and our fleet by them; and because they should not be in peace there, to refresh their water or to have conference with those of the Duke of Parma's party, my lord Admiral, with firing of ships, determined to remove them; as he did, and put them to the seas; in which broil the chief galleasse spoiled her rudder, and so rode ashore near the town of Calais, where she was possessed of our men, but so aground as she could not be brought away.

That morning, being Monday, the 29th of July, we followed the Spaniards; and all that day had with them a long and great fight, wherein there was great valour showed generally of our company. In this battle there was spent very much of our powder and shot; and so the wind began to blow westerly, a fresh gale, and the Spaniards put themselves somewhat to the northward, where we follow and keep company with them. . . . Now this fleet is here, and very forcible, and must be waited upon with all our force, which is little enough. There would be an infinite quantity of powder and shot provided, and continually sent abroad, without the which great hazard may grow to our country; for this is the greatest and strongest combination, to my understanding, that ever was gathered in Christendom. Therefore I wish it of all hands to be mightily and diligently looked unto and cared for.

The men have been long unpaid and need relief. I pray your lordship that the money that should have gone to Plymouth may now be sent to Dover. August now cometh in, and this coast will spend ground tackle, cordage, canvas and victuals; all which would be sent to Dover in good plenty. With these things and God's blessing our kingdom may be preserved; which being neglected, great hazard may come. I write to your lordship briefly and plainly. Your wisdom and experience is great; but this is a matter far passing all that hath been seen in our time or long before. And so praying to God for a happy deliverance from the malicious and dangerous practice of our enemies, I humbly take my leave. From the sea, aboard the *Victory*, the last of July, 1588.

The Spaniards take their course for Scotland; my lord doth follow them. I doubt not, with God's favour, we shall impeach their landing. There must be order for victual and money, powder and shot, to be sent after us.

Your lordship's humbly to command,
John Hawkyns.

When the fleet came home, the ballad-makers of London swamped the Stationer's Office for licenses to print ditty after ditty acclaiming the English seaman and the queen's navy. The country's taverns resounded to endless verses, rendered with beery enthusiasm:

> Come sound up your trumpets and beat up your drums,
>> And let's go to sea with a valiant cheer,
> In search of a mightie vast navy of ships,
>> The like has not been for these fifty long year.
>>> Raderer two, tandaro te,
>>> Raderer, tandorer, tan do te.

Queen Elizabeth proclaimed a day of thanksgiving, and Hakluyt describes how she "imitating the ancient Roman, rode into London in triumph, in regard of her owne and her subjects glorious deliverance. For being attended upon very solemnely by all the principall estates and officers of her Realme, she was carried thorow her sayd City of London in a triumphant chariot, and in robes of triumph, from her Palace unto the Cathedrall Church of Saint Paul, out of which the ensignes and colours of the vanquished Spaniards hung displayed. And all the citizens of London in their Liveries stood on either side of the street, by their several Companies, with their ensignes and banners: and the streets were hanged on both sides with Blew cloth, which, together with the aforesaid banners, yeelded a very stately and gallant prospect."

On the docks of the east coast, however, the spectacle was different. Lord Howard described it to Burghley: "My Lord, Sickness and mortality begin wonderfully to grow amongst us; and it is most pitiful to see, here at Margate, how the men, having no place to receive them into here, die in the streets. I am driven myself to come aland, to see them bestowed in some lodging; and the best I can get is barns and such outhouses; and the relief is small that I can provide for them here. It would grieve a man's heart to see them that have served so valiantly to die so miserably."

Daily sight of these miseries afflicted Hawkins at the same time that the Lord Treasurer, in almost daily messages, plagued him with the cost-conscious queen's insistence on the speediest of demobilizations.

Hawkins had always been exceptionally mindful of the nation's mariners. In 1585, fortified as ever by the irrefutable statistics of the mercantile accountant, he had got them a raise: he showed Burghley that if seamen's wages were stepped up from the current 6/8 a month to 10/- (and officers' wages accordingly) the quality of men offering to serve would be so much improved that a ship's company of 250 would be able to do much more than one of 300 paid at present rates. Smaller crews would mean smaller expenditures on victuals, and smaller cargo space for storing them. Using the 500-ton *Lion* for illustration, Hawkins pointed out that at the going rate of 23/4 for wages and victuals for one

Sir John Hawkins holding a captain's baton.

man per month, the cost of a crew of 300 worked out to £350; at the rate he proposed, 28/-, the *Lion* would have one good man per two tons of ship's weight as contrasted with a ragtag-and-bobtail crew of one man for every one and two-thirds tons, and the cost would be the same. Hawkins carried his point. But as the Armada crews were dismissed, calculation of amounts due and receipt of funds to pay them took time; meanwhile, the men were destitute.

In one of his letters to Burghley, Hawkins mentioned the discomfort he was enduring due to a breaking cable having struck one of his legs. Far more serious accidents at sea, crippling mariners beyond capacity for further employment, were common occurrences. Hawkins founded a seamen's hospital in Chatham in 1592, and he and Drake together set up the Chatham Chest (its strongbox can still be seen in Greenwich) for financial aid to the disabled.

Once demobilization was accomplished, Hawkins, in the autumn of 1588, sought Burghley's aid in obtaining Elizabeth's permission to retire from the Navy Board. She was far too shrewd to let a good man go: in February 1594 he was still petitioning for release.

During that time, Hawkins did have occasional respite from his shipyard duties. In 1590, with Frobisher as his vice admiral, he took a squadron to the Portuguese coast. Two years later, though he did not go himself, he sent out his ship *Dainty* as one of the privateers under Sir John Burgh lying in wait for Spanish treasure; she was in the action when the Portuguese carrack *Madre de Dios* was captured, bulging with Oriental cargo. But in the jamboree of riotous spoliation that followed the fight and continued all the way to Dartmouth harbor, the *Dainty* was left out: she had been dismasted before the carrack surrendered and had to limp home for repair without sharing in the loot.

The next year, however, the *Dainty* was herself again, and Hawkins's only son, Richard, captained her on a voyage intended as a further English thrust into the Far East via the route Drake had pioneered. Richard was then about thirty. As captain of the galliot *Duck*, he had joined in Drake's raid in the Caribbean in 1585, and upon the approach of the Armada in 1588 he had captained the *Swallow* out of Plymouth as part of the western squadron of the fleet. In 1593 he rounded the Horn successfully in the *Dainty*, then raided Valparaiso, and captured various prizes on his way north up the coast. But at San Mateo, after an engagement in which he was badly wounded, he became a Spanish prisoner, held first in Lima and then in Spain; he did not see England again until 1602. Knighted on his return, he became a true Hawkins of Plymouth: M.P. for the borough, Admiral of Devon, and vice admiral under Sir Robert Mansell on an expedition against the Barbary pirates in 1620.

The year that this last of the great Hawkinses died, 1622, was the year of publication of the book he wrote during his long captivity: *Observations in his Voiage into the South Sea*. The book bespeaks the Renaissance Man: he decorates his relation of his voyage with exact and vivid accounts of the natural world on the shores his ship was passing, and ranges from these acutely observed minutiae to broad sweeps of comprehension of the significance of the round globe as first encompassed in his time. And scattered along the way are reminiscences of moments in his family's past when the procedural niceties of medieval chivalry were still regarded as importantly enforceable:

I being of tender yeares, there came a Fleete of *Spaniards* of aboue fiftie sayle of Shippes, bound for *Flaunders*, to fetch the Queene, *Donna Anna de Austria*, last wife to *Philip* the second of *Spaine*, which entred betwixt the Iland and the Maine, without vayling their Top-sayles, or taking in of their Flags: which my Father, Sir *Iohn Hawkins*, (Admirall of a Fleete of her Maiesties Shippes, then ryding in *Catt-water*) perceiving, commanded his Gunner to shoot at the flagge of the Admirall, that they might thereby see their error: which notwithstanding, they persevered arrogantly to keepe displayed; wherevpon the Gunner at the next shott, lact the Admirall through and through, whereby the *Spaniards* finding that the matter beganne to grow to earnest, tooke in their Flags and Topsayles, and so ranne to an Anchor.

For father and son, Richard's departure on his voyage of 1593 was a last farewell. Two years after the *Dainty's* sailing, Sir John was paired with Sir Francis Drake on an expedition on which their contrasting temperaments could only lead to mutual ruin. As co-captains, they were sent out to the Caribbean, essentially to repeat the raid that Drake had conducted in 1585, but this time with a large military contingent, whose objective was to take both Nombre de Dios, on the east side of the Isthmus, and Panama, on the west, and thereby cut the connection between the source of Philip's New World wealth and the ships that carried it to Europe.

No two men had more greatly furthered the rise of Elizabeth's emerging empire, but no two differed more widely in the style of what they did. Hawkins was always a meticulous and careful planner, thoughtful of future consequences; age had now slowed his natural caution until one contemporary called him "old and wary, entering into matters with so leaden a foot that the other's meat would be eaten before his spit could come to the fire." Drake was an intuitive seizer of unplanned opportunities, daring the unintended, accomplishing the impossible by means of the unexpected. Increasing age accentuated their differences: Hawkins was near his mid-sixties; Drake was in his latter fifties. At the very start of the voyage, when Drake wanted to attack the Canaries and Hawkins thought it unnecessary, "the fire which lay hid in their stomachs began to break forth," as one of the military men observed. The fire was not put out, and the voyage perished in its ashes. First the elder, then the younger, died and was buried at sea.

On his last day, in his ship's cabin, Hawkins added an accountant's codicil to his will. Foreseeing the ruin of the expedition, and the cost implicit in the ruin to the queen, his last act was to settle his books so far as he was able. The fellow voyager who brought Elizabeth word of his death said that Hawkins knew her to have a considerable sum of his in her keeping; to the relinquishment of this he now added £2,000, "the best amends his poor ability could then stretch unto."

III

Searchers for a Northwest Passage

Y THE MID-1560S, EXPECTATIONS OF FINDING A
Northeast Passage to the Orient had been exhausted. Exploration north of Europe had enabled London merchants
to open commerce with Russia; a few determined traders
had pushed down from the north all the way to Turkey and Persia; and a
few intrepid voyagers had wintered on the Arctic island of Novaya
Zemlya and performed unbelievable feats of repairing broken rudders on
ships clogged with ice. But a Northeast Passage across the entire continent had been proved not to exist as a practical route for merchants.

So, swinging around 180 degrees, mercantile interest turned to the
northwest. Hope of a way in that direction was buoyed by a mistaken
assumption that the climate of North America might be comparable to
that of England. The latitude of London was 51.30° north, that of St.
John's, Newfoundland, chief port of the fisheries, was 47.34° north. The
transatlantic effect of the Gulf Stream was as yet unrecognized; only
gradually did the difference in temperature between the two shores of the
northern Atlantic become understood. So in the latter 1570s, London
money financed a group of voyages for exploration north and west of
Newfoundland's Grand Banks, long familiar to western European fishing fleets.

The three captains who made nearly simultaneous attempts to find a
Northwest Passage were friends: Martin Frobisher, Humphrey Gilbert,
and John Davis. The first to go, Frobisher, was backed on the initiative of
Michael Lok, a much-traveled young man whose father, a former sheriff
of London and a wealthy merchant friend of Sir Thomas Gresham, was
well able to stimulate enthusiasm at the Royal Exchange.

Through Lok's good offices, two tiny barks, the *Gabriel* and the

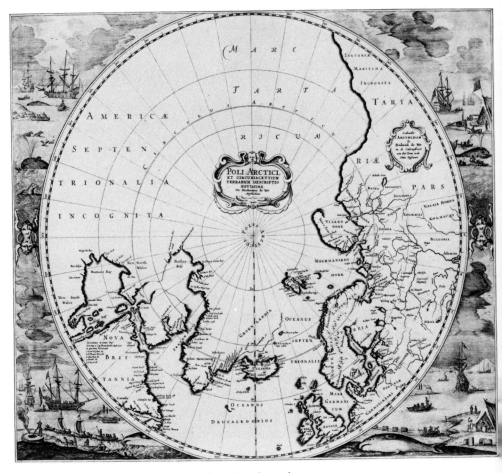

Map of the Arctic regions, c. 1590.

Michael, and a pinnace sailed from London in June 1576. They first followed the familiar route toward the Newfoundland fisheries; along the way, as not infrequently happened on these voyages, the *Michael* turned about and sailed home. With only the *Gabriel* and the pinnace, Frobisher continued north, passing Cape Farewell at the tip of Greenland, and then turned northwest. His next landfall was at the opening in Baffin Island now known as Frobisher Bay. Assuming that this entrance led to the Passage, he went no further and arrived home in October to announce that he had located the promised connection to the East.

If one of his ship's company had not picked up a rock on an island— perhaps Lok's Island at the entrance to the bay—Frobisher's further expeditions might have fared better. In London, the rock was held to contain firm evidence that the expedition had found gold. Envy of the Inca mines that annually enriched Spain excited hopes in all early American exploration by the English; Frobisher's London backers quickly shifted their interest from a potential passage to a nugget in the hand.

Queen Elizabeth became an investor, with £1,000 and her 180-ton ship *Aid*; Michael Lok became governor of the new Company of Cathay; Frobisher was sent back to dig ore. He loaded up, and returned.

By 1578, the rock had set off a gold rush. Though assayists were still analyzing the diggings of the year before and had come to no conclusion regarding their content, a fleet of fifteen sail was dispatched; it carried colonists and supplies to start a settlement that would remain at the site after the next load of ore was carried back to England.

Everything went wrong. On the way out, the weather was terrible: the bark *Dennis*, whose cargo contained many of the colonists' winter supplies, foundered on the way. Frobisher's own navigator overshot the site; he sailed west on a line too far south and reached the great opening, named for Hendrik Hudson thirty years later, that offered every promise of being a Northwest Passage. London's abandonment of interest in exploration is symbolized by the name Frobisher gave the body of water he had entered: Mistaken Bay. At the end of the season the expedition came home, without leaving a colony behind, to find that while it was away the bubble had burst. The assayists had finished their analysis, and

Sir Martin Frobisher, seeker of a Northwest Passage, and officer on many voyages in the Tudor age.

Compton Castle.

their conclusion was NO GOLD. The collapse left Michael Lok's name burdened with some £20,000 of company debt.

At the time that Frobisher's backers were demonstrating that their desire for immediate gain had supplanted their desire for a western trade-route, Sir Humphrey Gilbert was preparing to sail under letters patent granted by the queen for "the Westerne Discovery of America and to plant a colony," and his younger brother Adrian was working on similar plans with their mutual boyhood friend, John Davis.

For two hundred years there had been Gilberts among Devon's upper gentry at Compton Castle, ever since the fourteenth-century Geoffrey Gilbert married Joan de Compton; her ancestors had already held the land for seven generations. The castle on this fortified farm, still the family residence, was rebuilt with additions by successive Gilberts, and completed, with its fortifications much as they are now, by the first quarter of the sixteenth century. The fourteenth-century Geoffrey Gilbert was a member of Parliament in 1326; the fifteenth-century Otho Gilbert was sheriff of Devon in 1475. The sixteenth-century family divided its time between two estates, Compton near Totnes and Greenway on the River Dart in the parish of Stoke Gabriel. It was at Greenway that the children of Sir Humphrey's generation were born.

Their mother was Katherine Champernoune of Modbury, Devon, a sister of Sir Arthur Champernoune, the county's Lord Lieutenant. By her first marriage, in 1531 to the sixteenth-century Otho Gilbert of Compton who died in 1547, she bore three sons who lived to maturity: John, sheriff of Devon in 1572 and the shire's vice admiral, whose brilliantly painted canopied tomb in Exeter Cathedral shelters recumbent figures of himself and his wife; Humphrey; and Adrian. When Katherine married again, she took as her second husband Walter Ralegh, Sr., of Hayes Barton, a farm near East Budleigh, and there in addition to a daughter, Margaret, bore two more sons, Walter and Carew. Hers was an impressive brood: four of the five boys, all except Adrian, received knighthoods from Elizabeth.

Their mother was named for her aunt Katherine, whose husband, Thomas Ashley, was a connection of the Boleyns. In Catholic Queen Mary's reign, the aunt was governess to the neglected Protestant princess Elizabeth; she continued in the household, as Mistress of the Robes, after the princess became queen. Through her, Humphrey Gilbert had his start. According to the seventeenth-century gossip John Aubrey, as a very young man Gilbert "was for a time not only in the Queen's service, but in her favour, who would often confer with him in matters of learning, and in all probability about his favorite studies of Cosmography and Navigation, which could not but be favorable to his fortunes in the succeeding part of his life, and entitle him to such marks of his Sovereign's favour as even his great merit would scarce have procured, if he had not been brought so early into her majesty's family."

So it was easy for Sir Humphrey Gilbert, when he returned from Ireland in 1576 bearing dispatches from Sir Henry Sidney, commander-in-chief of Her Majesty's forces there, to gain the queen's ear. Sidney had just knighted Gilbert on the field and commended him in a letter to Her Majesty:

For the Colonel [Gilbert] I cannot say enough. The highways are now made free where no man might travel undespoiled. The gates of the cities and towns are now left open, where before they were continually shut or

Sir Humphrey Gilbert.

guarded with armed men. There was none that was a rebel of any force but has submitted himself, entered into bond, and delivered hostages, the arch-rebel James FitzMaurice only excepted, who is become a bush-beggar, not having 20 knaves to follow him, and yet this is not the most or the best that he hath done; for the estimation that he hath won to the name of Englishmen there, before almost not known, exceedeth all the rest; for he in battle brake so many of them, where he showed how far our soldiers in valour surpassed these rebels, and he in his own person any man he had. The name of Englishman is more terrible now to them than the sight of a hundred was before. For all this I had nothing to present him with but the honour of knighthood, which I gave him.

(Sidney avoided mention of Gilbert's measures that exemplified the practices of the times—as a warning to the rebels, the heads of those killed in an engagement were thereafter placed to flank the path to his post of command.)

When not abroad on military service—he had suffered a defeat on impossible terrain when helping Dutch rebels against Spain's occupation of the Netherlands—Gilbert had for some years lived in London. In 1570, he married Anne Aucher, for whom he named his flagship; they dwelt in Limehouse to be near the shipping district. The youngest of his six sons, Ralegh Gilbert, his eventual heir at Compton, continued the family interest in North America as one of the eight patentees who founded Jamestown in 1607.

In the '60s, Gilbert had begun circulating a manuscript composed to attract Elizabeth's attention to northwestern exploration. It began with the assertion that "it were the onely way for our princes, to possesse ye welth of all the East partes (as they tearme them) of the worlde, which is infinite . . . which would be a great advancement to our Countrie, wonderful enriching to our Prince, and unspeakable commodities to all the inhabitants of Europe." He now presented a printed version of his *Discourse* to Elizabeth, with a map drawn specially for the occasion and a request for letters patent to proceed.

In arguing for a combination of settlement in America with further exploration of a way to the Orient, Gilbert promised betterment of several kinds:

Since the world is a globe, a northern route would be shorter, and therefore cheaper, than any open to Spain; if taken from North American settlements it would be far shorter still.

Eastern trade would increase the number of large-sized ships in England's navy, train additional crews, and give more constant employment to seamen.

An all-English route would save customs duties and port charges, permitting merchants to sell goods at home at lower prices, and to bring home hitherto unavailable goods, and goods that now have to be procured from Europe.

The potentates ruling the East, in their reported magnificence, would become purchasers of rich clothing, and buoy the sagging English cloth market.

Emigration from England to the colonies would lessen the currently troublesome domestic unemployment: the realm would no longer be "combred with loyterers, vagabonds, and such like idle persons," and poor men's children could be put to work making the trifles that do well in the North American Indian trade.

Gilbert prudently ended his argument with a standard assurance dear to the queen: his discovery would be "without injurie done to any Christian prince, by crossing them in any of their used trades, whereby they might take any just occasion of offence."

As soon as he had received the letters patent granted him on June 2, 1578, Gilbert began to assemble a fleet, but he had a hard time getting away. The eleven sail he led out of Dartmouth in September ran into gales that drove them all the way east to the Isle of Wight. When he tried again in October, he was blown back once more. By that time he had lost the companionship of Sir Henry Knollys, who after bickering about plans withdrew his four ships from the expedition. When Gilbert finally departed, it was November 19 and his fleet numbered only seven: his own 250-ton *Ann Ager*, the 150-ton *Hope of Greenway*, captained by Carew Ralegh, the 100-ton *Falcon*, captained by Walter Ralegh, the 110-ton *Red Lion* under Miles Morgan, and three smaller vessels. And when he came back at the end of February he had lost a ship and accomplished little.

His return was greeted with a charge of piracy, brought by King Philip's ambassador, Bernardino de Mendoza, who had derogated Gilbert's Portuguese-born, Spanish-trained pilot, Simon Fernandez, as "a great rogue, who knows that coast well, and has given them much information about it." The Privy Council considered the charge, restricted Gilbert's license, and sent him back to Ireland for another term of military service.

But his project did not die—it was saved by the Privy Council's adventurous member, Sir Francis Walsingham. By April 1582, Gilbert had new plans. He financed this venture by selling overseas real estate in Baccalaos, the name given to the land along the shores of Labrador and Newfoundland; a company had been formed with Walsingham as its chief patron.

Since Gilbert anticipated that the colony would be a complete society, not just a mercantile entrepôt, he had given great thought to its physical layout, to the structure of its government, and to the powers to be exercised by those in charge, expressed in the will that he prudently drew up before departure:

The powers of the governor were to be close to absolute, though an elected council of thirteen was to advise him on defense. At Gilbert's own death, all revenues were to be reserved to his heir, though a third was to be paid to his wife during his heir's minority and a fifth, subsequently. She herself was to receive a fifty-square-mile seigniory that would become a perquisite of the governor's wife forever; each of his sons was likewise to receive such a seigniory, and his daughters one of twenty square miles, to be ruled by them, with a fee paid to the general revenue.

Every colonist sent by the mother country was to bring with him specified quantities of seed for initial sowings of grain, and a hatchet, a pickaxe, a saw, and a spade. He was to be given a lease of sixty acres of land, to run for three lives, and adequate supplies of wood. Gentlemen who brought colonists with them were to receive headrights of 400 acres per immigrant, and each immigrant a holding of six acres.

As contributions to the common defense, rulers of seigniories were to be responsible for furnishing an armed horseman; tenants of sixty acres were to maintain a longbow and arrows and own a sword, dagger, and shield; tenants of twenty-four acres to keep a fighting man in addition to themselves. Lessors of 2,000 acres were to keep either a horse for the wars or two men until a sufficient number of horses were in the country. In addition, a tax of a halfpenny sterling per acre was to be levied for support of the colony's army and navy.

Gilbert's plan for the physical appearance of the colony recalled the villages of Devon:

Parishes were to be blocked out on three-mile squares, with an Anglican church at their center. Ministers should receive three hundred acres, as near to the church as possible, in addition to their tithes. Holding more than one benefice—a common practice in England—was forbidden, and an absence of more than six months would cancel a charge. Suitably larger acreages were to be reserved for bishops and archbishops.

Gilbert's strong belief in education—when in London he had drawn up elaborate plans for "an Achademie" to be founded under Elizabeth's patronage—appeared in his provision for lectures and schools. Other institutions would support maimed and aged soldiers and sailors, and aged clergy.

Such was the proposed outline for the first English town in the New World.

In preparing his 1583 voyage, Gilbert had a further objective in mind: to conduct a ceremony that would clear up the matter of title to Newfoundland. The good fishing on the Grand Banks attracted fishing boats from Spain, Portugal, France, and the Scandinavian countries as well as England. But Newfoundland had been seen and described by both John and Sebastian Cabot when in the employ of earlier Tudor rulers; there should be a reassertion of English sovereignty now that the area had taken on international importance.

On June 11, 1583, Gilbert sailed in the 120-ton *Delight*, with Richard Clarke as master; with him were the 40-ton *Swallow*, captained by Maurice Browne, the 40-ton *Golden Hinde of Weymouth*, owned and captained by Edward Hayes, and the little 10-ton *Squirrel*. Present at the start was the 200-ton *Bark Ralegh*, owned and equipped by Gilbert's half brother, but a few days out she withdrew on the grounds of sickness in the crew. Her departure robbed the expedition of its largest ship, and its correspondingly largest cargo.

Off St. John's, Newfoundland, the fleet came near to losing the *Delight* through negligent seamanship; she grounded, and only with luck was backed off on the next high tide. Some days later, Gilbert summoned the port's inhabitants and carried out his political objective. After formally proclaiming the sovereignty of the queen, he bulwarked permanent recognition of Elizabeth's possession by erecting a pillar with a lead plaque bearing the royal arms.

Though once again a sample of ore, said this time to contain traces of silver, was picked up, the expedition was not diverted. After the St. John's ceremony, sickness having spread through the fleet, Gilbert sent the *Swallow* home with the ailing, transferred Maurice Browne to captain the *Delight*, and set out to explore more southerly shores as possible sites for further settlement. He himself, because he would be making frequent landings, sailed in the *Squirrel* to take advantage of her shallow draft.

Nine days later, the *Delight* was leading the little procession when William Coxe, master of the *Golden Hinde*, suddenly saw sand beneath his ship. A quick signal warned the others, but for the *Delight* the warning came too late. Her second grounding was fatal.

She broke up rapidly, while Gilbert witnessed the death of close to a hundred of his men; among the lost was the Hungarian poet Parmenius, who had written an ode to the voyage before it started and anticipated publishing a full account after his return. In an early instance of such heroism, Captain Browne—refusing an offer of aid—went down with his ship. Only fourteen of those on board survived, in a tiny one-and-a-half-ton pinnace built at St. John's; her sole contents were a single oar— no food, no water. Sixteen men were in her when she pulled away, one of them being Richard Clarke, the *Delight*'s master. Two died during the coming ordeal. Day by day, for a week, Clarke kept up his companions' courage by promising an imminent landfall. Finally ashore, they feasted on wild pease and berries, and watched for a sail. Eventually, a French fisherman rescued them.

Meanwhile, Gilbert had turned his two remaining ships toward England. The North Atlantic soon surged in autumn anger. From the *Golden Hinde*, Edward Hayes importuned Gilbert to move to the larger ship: the little *Squirrel* was not up to such a sea. Gilbert refused: "I will not forsake my little company going homeward, with whom I have passed so many storms and perils."

They reached the Azores intact, only to run into still more terrible weather as they turned north toward England; after dark, night after night, St. Elmo's fire flickered on the yardarms. About midnight on September 9, one last enormous wave overarched the *Squirrel* and sailed her under; by morning light, those on the *Golden Hinde* saw they were alone. One of William Sanderson's men who had traveled supercargo on her set down the expedition's story.

In his *Discourse* Gilbert had written: ". . . he is not worthy to live at all, that for fear or danger of death shunneth his countrey's service and his own honour." His decision to stay on the *Squirrel* can be read as a matter of "his own honour." He may have been proving something, for when this voyage was in preparation, he had received from the queen what might be taken for a challenge. Her Majesty sanctioned the undertaking—she sent him as a token a small gold anchor with a pearl at its peak—but at the same time she urged him not to go on it himself; he was, she said, "a man noted for no good hap at sea."

The Gilbert family interest in the Northwest Passage did not die with Sir Humphrey. His younger brother Adrian was deep in such projects with the learned and mysterious John Dee, who had gained notoriety as a mathematician, astronomer, and astrologer. Dee's diary for the years 1579–82 notes various consultations between the two of them and Gilbert's boyhood playmate, John Davis, who lived at Sandridge on the Dart near the Gilbert home at Greenway, as well as several sessions at which they briefed Sir Francis Walsingham.

While Adrian applied for and received letters patent, his own seafaring is unrecorded. But he was one of Davis's backers, supplying the 50-ton *Sunshine* and the 35-ton *Moonshine*. During the sailing seasons of 1585–87, Davis searched consistently and single-mindedly for the Northwest Passage whose existence was revealed only in 1851 by Collinson and McClure, and not traversed in a single season until 1905, by Roald Amundsen in his *Gjoa*.

In 1585 Davis's first landfall was along the eternally icebound east coast of Greenland. He turned south to sail around Cape Farewell and ascend the west coast, which he named "Desolation." Some leagues to the north, he found green shores and rested on them; then he headed northwest. Believing an estuary that now bears his name to be the entry to the Passage, he was disappointed to reach its western shore—it is part of Baffin Island. But the gulf that was shortly to be named for George Clifford, Lord Cumberland, opened to the west so widely that after penetrating it for a considerable distance, he returned home full of hope.

The next year and the year after, he pushed further north up Davis Strait into Baffin Bay. In a little bark of twenty tons—he had left his other ships at the cod fishery—he advanced as far as 73° north in ice-free water, and turned west. He was less than a degree below Lancaster Sound, the opening over the top of Baffin Island that begins the actual Northwest Passage, when ice floes blocked him—the air was loud with the "rowling together of islands of ice"—and a strong north wind forced him south again.

Davis continued to believe in the existence of the Passage he had almost entered—in 1595 he published *The Worlde's Hydrographicall Description* giving his reasons—but after his series of thorough searches the hope for a usable channel for trade had to be abandoned. He had placed on the northern land an enduring series of names of other true believers—the Gilbert and the Cumberland Sound, Mount Raleigh, Cape Walsingham, and Sanderson-his-Hope. But the same difficulties that had caused the voyages for a Northeast Passage to end with that of Arthur Pett and Charles Jackman in 1580 had been recognized as applying in this direction: ice, ice, and more ice had encased mercantile hopes for a feasible route. In the absence of a northern path to the glittering Oriental trade, merchants' assessments of possible gains in the New World turned to more drab prospects. Gilbert's assertion of English possession of Newfoundland and his detailed plans for a colony envisaged a commerce in such prosaic but not unprofitable commodities as codfish.

However, if there was no way north to the Orient, there were proven ways in other directions. Though direct competition with Spain appeared to be the price of using them, English merchants were willing to try. There were two possibilities: the route around Africa's Cape of Good Hope, originally pioneered by the Portuguese, and the route across South America's Horn, discovered by Magellan and recently traversed by Drake and Cavendish. On both courses Davis accumulated a record of navigational experience with which only that of Drake is comparable.

Before he undertook a new series of distant ventures, he took part in a number closer to home. He returned from the Arctic in time to join the battle against the Armada—he is thought to be the John Davis who commanded the *Black Dog*, tender to Lord Howard's flagship. For two years thereafter, he served in the squadrons operating between England and the Azores, searching for homebound Spanish fleets. But in 1591, when Thomas Cavendish started around the Horn for the second time, Davis went along.

They got no further than the western end of the Strait of Magellan, where the violent storms that lay in wait for exiting ships lashed into and separated them. Three times, Davis succeeded in emerging from the strait; three times, he was forced back into it by gales. He returned to Port Desire on the east coast, and after a long wait for Cavendish, who had headed homeward and died en route, he came back to England in 1593.

On arrival, Davis was greeted by the information that his wife—her name was Faith—had taken a lover in his absence. The man made a business of harassing Davis with lawsuits until the abandoned husband found a champion in Ralegh.

Over the next two years, Davis turned his energies toward forwarding some ideas for improving English navigation—he was in hearty accord with Samuel Purchas's declaration, made a few years later, that "the sea yields the world to the world by this art of arts, navigation." In 1595 he put on the market a new invention: a far more accurate adaptation of the cross-staff all captains carried, enabling them to estimate their latitude by determining the angle formed by the horizon and the elevation of the noonday sun. With the old model, an observer had to hold the staff so that one edge of its cross-piece was on the horizon and the other at the center of the sun, forcing the observer to look directly at the sun to set it. Davis's new back-staff, held over the shoulder, allowed a navigator to calculate the angle by a beam of the sun's light passing through two sights on its upper bar to intersect with the horizontal line. Comparison of the angle as determined by either instrument with tables carried in the chart room would show him where his ship was.

That same year, Davis published a seaman's manual whose popularity quickly outdistanced previous publications—over the next fifty years, it became the standard description of the main instruments a captain should take with him, and of their uses. His *Seaman's Secrets* ran through eight editions and was to be found in the great cabin of most ships.

In 1596 Davis was back at sea on the Cadiz expedition, where he seems to have been master of Ralegh's *Warspite* in the attack for which Sir Walter was strategist. Then the young earl of Essex, co-captain general on that occasion, advised him to take service with the Dutch and see what he could learn from and about their increasingly numerous visits to the Far East. Davis accepted the advice, and obtained a commission on the *Leeuw* (*Lion*), under Captain Cornelius Houtman, who had made the first Dutch trip over the old Portuguese route in 1595. With her companion, the *Lioness*, Davis's ship sailed from Flushing in 1598.

En route and after arrival, one fight followed another. At Saldanha Bay, just before rounding the Cape of Good Hope, they lost men in a fight with natives. After stops in Madagascar and the Maldive Islands southwest of India, they stayed for some months at Acheen on the west coast of Sumatra, but the king, initially friendly, turned on them. His men took the *Lioness* and attacked the *Lion*. Firing from her barricaded

taine large degrées, but also to auoyd the vncertainic of $\bar{y}$ sight, by disoz-
derly placing of the staffe to the eye, which demonstration I haue found, &
haue had the instrument in pzactise, aswell vnder the Sun, as in other climates, but because it hath a large demostratiõ, with manifold vses, I here
omit to manifest the same, purposing to wzite a particular treatise thereof,
notwithstãoing his fozme & vse, by picture I haue thought good to expzesse.

This staffe is a yard long, hauing 2. halfe crosses, the one circular, the o-
ther straight, the longest not 14. inches, yet this staffe doth contain the
whole 90. degrées, the shortest degrée being an inch & $\frac{1}{4}$ long, wherein the
minuts are particularly & very sensibly laid down, by which staffe not regarding the parallax of your sight, noz looking vpon the Sunne, but onely
vpon the Hozizon, the Suns height is most pzecisely knowne, as well and
as easily in the Zenith, as in any other part of the heauen. Then which instrument (in my opinion) the Seaman shall not finde any so good, & in all
Climates of so great certainty, the inuention & demonstration whereof I
may boldly chalenge to appertaine vnto my selfe (as a poztiõ of the talent
which God hath bestowed vpõ me) I hope without abuse oz offence to any,

Back-staff for improved determination of latitude, invented by
John Davis in 1595.

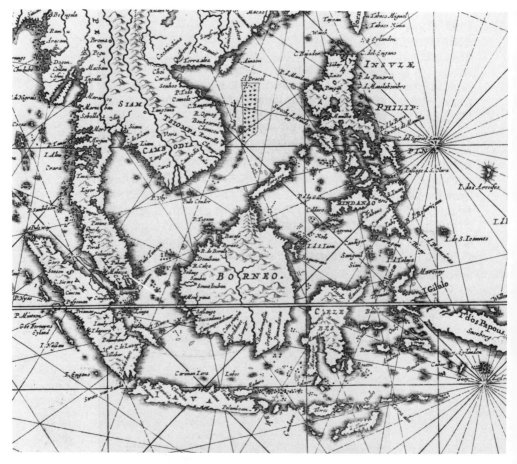

Detail from the Blaeus' *New Atlas*, showing the region of Southeast Asia
where John Davis went on his last voyage.

stern castle, Davis, another Englishman, and a Frenchman succeeded in getting the *Lioness* back, but before the ships broke free, upwards of seventy-five of their men had been killed, and the cargo they had collected, including pepper, was ruined. Still another fight, against Portuguese galleys, awaited them before they returned to Flushing in 1600.

With the experience he had accumulated, Davis came back to England, ready to take a place in his own country's entrance into the Far East—the initial English trading voyage via the Cape of Good Hope had gone out in 1591 and returned after a highly profitable sojourn in 1594. By 1599, London merchants had raised substantial capital—some £30,000—and at the end of 1600 Elizabeth had granted a charter for a company to break the Dutch monopoly on the spice trade, giving "The Governor and Company of Merchants trading into the East Indies" both governmental and economic powers that made history in the region for well over two hundred years. When its first fleet sailed from Woolwich in 1601 for a highly successful two-year voyage, Davis was its admiral.

On his return, a quick turnaround set him off again in 1604 as pilot of the 210-ton *Tiger*. After a year of visiting Oriental markets, his merchandising accomplished, he coasted along Sumatra on his way home. When his ship reached the tiny island of Bandung, between the tip of the Malay peninsula and the Sumatra shore, he came routinely to anchor.

Next to him was a disabled junk crowded with Japanese. They were not refugees; they were pirates. In a surprise attack, they leaped onto the *Tiger*, and only with difficulty were driven off. In the course of the foray, Davis was murdered.

By the time Elizabeth died, her merchants and her seamen had combined to find an equivalent of the passages to the northeast and the northwest that they had begun to seek half a century earlier. The route opened by Vasco da Gama was no longer a private perquisite of Spain; the new rivals for its exploitation were the English and the Dutch.

Davis's double measure of experience could well have been the inspiration of a poem that Thomas Weelkes set to music in 1600 for Englishmen to sing:

Thule, the period of Cosmographie
Doth vaunt of Hecla, whose sulphurious fire
Doth melt the frozen Clime and thaw the skie—
Trinacrian Aetna's flames ascend not higher;

    These things seem wondrous, yet more wondrous I
    Whose hart with feare doth freeze, with love doth fry.

The Andalusian Merchant that returnes
Laden with Cutchinele and China dishes,
Reports in Spaine how strangely Fogo burnes
Amidst an Ocean full of flying fishes;

    These things seem wondrous, yet more wondrous I
    Whose hart with feare doth freeze, with love doth fry.

IV

The Grenville Clarion

FTER SIR HUMPHREY GILBERT'S DEATH, SIR Walter Ralegh applied for what was essentially a continuance of his half brother's letters patent, and received confirmation in the spring of 1584 in time to send a pair of young men from his household to America to find a site for a colony. The young men were Philip Amadas of Plymouth (perhaps a Hawkins relative) and Arthur Barlowe, who wrote a report about what they found.

Until Elizabeth declined to let him leave court, Ralegh had fully expected to lead a colony to the spot they recommended in the spring of the following year; instead, when the five ships and two pinnaces of the expedition departed Plymouth on April 9, 1585, the captain general was his cousin Sir Richard Grenville.

Among forebears of the great Devon navigators, the Grenville family held social pride of place. The first Sir Richard de Granville came to England with his kinsman William the Conqueror, and within a few years the family was possessed of the West Country manors of Bideford and Kilkhampton—the multi-arched entrance portal of their parish church, St. James at Kilkhampton, is a masterpiece of Norman architecture. These holdings gave them a firm footing on each side of the northern end of the dividing line between Cornwall and Devon: the Devon town of Bideford was the site of one of their residences, their place of business, and their port; their great house was at Stowe in Cornwall, some thirty miles west. In the Bideford Church of St. Mary is a vast wooden tower screen from the late sixteenth century, carved with panels in which the Grenville blazon displays its three clarions. (The clarion was a blown instrument of which Chaucer said: "For in fight and blodshedinge / Ys used gladly clarionynge.") The clarions are repeated on carved pew ends at Kilkhampton. The Grenvilles were patrons of both benefices.

The sixteenth-century Richard Grenville who was Ralegh's cousin was the son of Roger, master of Henry VIII's 700-ton *Mary Rose* when she went down with all hands in sight of the sovereign, in The Solent off Southsea Castle during the attempted invasion by the French in 1545. At the time, Richard was a three- or four-year-old child. A decade later, he became the heir of his grandfather, another Sir Richard, who had been a canny purchaser of monastic lands and who willed the boy the estate of Buckland Abbey, a few miles above Plymouth. Some years after the grandson came of age, he made it his residence; he was Devon's sheriff in 1577, the year that he was knighted.

In the early 1570s, however, Grenville lived in London in St. Olave's parish, Southwark, close by London Bridge; the house, an imposing stone-and-timber residence formerly belonging to the abbot of St. Augustus, Canterbury, was owned by his relatives, the St. Legers. From there, with other West Country gentlemen, he pressed upon the queen an unusual plan for a trade route to the Orient: their request for letters patent argued for a passage, with settlements to be set up along it, quite different from that proposed by Gilbert in the *Discourse* he was currently circulating. The Grenville group's suggested alternative was described in *A Discourse concerninge a Straighte to be discovered towarde the northweste passinge to Cathaia, and the Orientall Indians, with a confutacion of their errour that thinke the discouerye thereof to be most conveniently attempted to the north of Baccalaos*. The plan was to round the Horn, enter the South Sea, sail up the west coast of South America, and continue north to enter the fabled Strait of Anian, believed to run directly to India from upper North America. Talk of the Pacific Ocean, once Drake had seen it in 1573, was in the air. Since no one after Magellan had rounded the Horn, Grenville was oblivious to the rigors of that passage, and he dismissed objection to the discomforts of his route's double exposure to equatorial heat by observing that English seamen were by now comfortably familiar with the first leg of his proposed way as far down as southern Brazil.

He proposed placing a colony at the River Plate, erecting fortifications at the Strait of Magellan, and locating other settlements on the southwestern South American coast. Such settlements, he observed,

Sir Richard Grenville in 1571.

would relieve current overpopulation in England, and their strategic military advantages were obvious.

In closing his request, he warmed Elizabeth's heart by declaring that he and his associates would finance the entire expense of the voyage. The queen issued the letters patent.

Grenville began extensive preparations. He, with William Hawkins and others, was a co-owner of the 240-ton *Castle of Comfort*, well known as a privateer in the Channel. He bought two additional ships, and began negotiations for more. A Spanish intelligence agent in London reported that he and Sir Arthur Champernoune, by then Vice Admiral of the West, were arming seven ships, four of them large: "The real design is not yet known, as there are so many plans afoot, but as they are going in this guise, they probably mean to sack some of the islands and lie in wait for the ships from the Indies and other merchantmen. They say they are taking with them a store hulk of 600 tons, with provisions, but I believe it is more likely to carry plunder than to take stores. They sail this month."

The plan was busily maturing when Grenville received dismaying news: Her Majesty had changed her mind. Chary of rousing the wrath of Philip, the queen had heard that existing Spanish settlements extended down the western coast of South America well below the mining areas of Peru. Grenville's colonies would therefore be in his domain, and Philip, though a Catholic, was undoubtedly a Christian king, entitled to be undisturbed within his recognized territories. So the voyage was disallowed.

Grenville was crushed. Supersensitive to his honor in an age of aristocratic sensitivity, he disengaged himself, not only from his associates but from the adventuring of the age. For the next few years, he lived as a private country gentleman, chiefly busying himself with the conversion of Buckland Abbey into a stately home. Unlike most reorganizers of ecclesiastical property, he did not pull the old structures down and use their materials in new designs. Except for its transepts, he left the monks' church intact: the outer walls remained as they were to form the exterior of his dwelling. The former choir became the great hall, and for

Buckland Abbey, where Grenville used the Cistercian monks' former
church for the external walls of his new house.

The carved plaster frieze in Buckland Abbey ordered by Sir Richard
Grenville to tell the story of his dismay when Queen Elizabeth cancelled
his letters patent for rounding the Horn and sailing to the Orient.

its decorated plaster frieze Grenville, with the personal attention that he lavished on all details, ordered a poignant autobiography. The hall's chief overmantel was conventional enough, a carefully balanced Renaissance design, displaying allegorical figures of Justice, Temperance, Prudence, and Fortitude, together with the date of completion of the work, 1576. But in the plaster frieze on the west wall, he permitted himself a romantic outburst, a revelation of his persistent bitterness and hurt at the queen's shattering of his dream. The scene carved there shows a knight withdrawn from the world. He has turned loose his great war-horse, taken off his armor, hung his shield on a branch of a tree, and seated himself beneath the tree with an hourglass and a skull, there to contemplate the transitory nature of life and the certainty of mortality.

Four years later, Drake's return from his circumnavigation reopened Grenville's wounds: the route the new national hero had taken was the one that he had been briefly granted for his own. While Drake had had no intent of colonization, he had rounded the Horn, sailed up the western coast of the Americas, and after failing to find the non-existent Strait of Anian, turned west, reached the Orient, and come laden home. With the lucrative prizes he had collected along the way this Devon yeoman's son had become a very rich man. At the award of his knighthood, the queen had graced his ship with her presence.

Grenville prepared to retire still further. Two Plymouth men, Christopher Harris and John Hele, came to him with an offer to buy Buckland. They were known to be the intermediaries whom Drake normally employed for his business affairs. Nevertheless, Grenville accepted their offer. He removed to Cornwall and Stowe, and thereafter his port was Bideford, whose incorporation he had procured in 1573. Within months, a large painting of Drake's new coat of arms decorated the wall above one of Buckland's overmantels.

For four long years, Grenville held to his self-imposed retirement. When he emerged, it was at the request of his cousin Walter Ralegh, who had just suffered a disappointment of his own. Ralegh was initiating colonization in America, the only objective in Grenville's former plan that Drake had not borrowed.

The proposed location was intriguing: Humphrey Gilbert had come to the conclusion that for a North American climate more comparable to that of England than the lands along the fiftieth parallel a site would have to be sought well to the south of Baccalaos, perhaps in the area known as Norembega (today's New England, from Maine south to Manhattan). Ralegh's chosen location was even further south, below Chesapeake Bay.

The climate of a colony there was apt to be hot, politically as well as geographically: its location would be a definite infringement of that extensive area which the Spanish called Florida. In the 1560s, when French Huguenots had put a settlement on the peninsula called Florida today, Spanish reaction had been swift and ruthless: the village John Hawkins succored had been rooted out, and some of its refugees had found their way to London. The Ralegh settlement was likely to become a test case too. So when Elizabeth decided she could not spare so captivating a subject as Ralegh from her court, Grenville accepted the assignment.

As captain general, he headed a fleet of seven ships gaily waved out of Plymouth harbor on April 8, 1585. His flagship was the *Tiger*, a loan from the queen, who had also allowed Ralegh four hundred pounds of gunpowder from the royal stores. The *Tiger* was a tough craft that remained in the Royal Navy long past the Armada and underwent many rebuildings; at this date she was probably rated at 200 tons. Next in size was Ralegh's own 140-ton *Roebuck*, named for the deer that topped the crest of his coat of arms; it was captained by John Clarke. The captain of the 100-ton *Lion* was George Raymond; the 50-ton *Elizabeth* was both owned and captained by Thomas Cavendish. Besides these there were three pinnaces, of which Ralegh's *Dorothie* is listed as departing with the expedition but not mentioned thereafter.

The fleet made a brave show as it passed the Eddystone and turned down the Channel. The course Grenville proposed to follow had become the standard route to the West Indies—south from England to the Canary Islands, then west to ride the Bahama current and catch the steady trade winds that blow up the west African coast and cross to the West Indies. But between him and the Canaries lay the waters west of

The *Tiger*, loaned by Queen Elizabeth, on which Grenville led the first English-speaking colony to America, sent out by Sir Walter Ralegh in 1585.

the Bay of Biscay, terrible in their anger, and angry when the fleet arrived. Grenville's ships could not stay together, and only the *Tiger* and the *Elizabeth* saw each other again in the course of the voyage, though each of the other large ships eventually reached the Outer Banks.

Captain Raymond's passage was a miserable affair: before he reached Jamaica his food supply was so utterly exhausted that he put a number of men ashore to fend for themselves. In mid-June, when he landed near the colony's proposed site, nobody was there; he left some thirty colonists—of whom only two later succeeded in joining Grenville—and took the *Lion* home. That Captain Clarke arrived is known only because his name is on a list of men whom Grenville took with him on an

Thomas Cavendish, who sailed his own *Elizabeth*
in the fleet that established Ralegh's 1585 colony on Roanoke Island
and who, the following year, became the second Englishman
to circumnavigate the world.

exploration of Pamlico Sound; in any event, the *Roebuck* survived to make further history.

Yet Grenville's *Tiger* fared well; even her log suffered no accident and was preserved by Hakluyt in his *Principall Voyages and Navigations*. In the *Tiger* with the captain general was the colony's governor-designate, Ralph Lane of Lympstone on the River Exe. Holding a minor post as equerry to the queen, he happened to be on a return from Ireland when the colony's officers were being selected; he brought with him a reputation as a difficult companion-in-arms. Also aboard was the colony's treasurer, Francis Brooke, a gentleman previously engaged in privateering. So were Thomas Harriot, an Oxford scientist, and John White, an artist; these two had been commissioned by Ralegh to record flora and fauna and Indian life in the vicinity of the colony. The two Indians, Wanchese and Manteo, who had come to England on the homeward voyage of Amadas and Barlowe, were now themselves homebound. The *Tiger* also accommodated the fleet's pilot, Portuguese-born, Spanish-trained Simon Fernandez; well familiar with the American coast, he had been Humphrey Gilbert's pilot before being signed on by Ralegh.

The ship enjoyed a rapid voyage over. Leaving the Canaries on April 14, she was in the West Indies by the first week of May. To give the ship-bound company a breather, Grenville anchored at the little island of Cotesa, south of Puerto Rico; he then moved across to Mosquito (Guayanilla) Bay for two serious purposes. In a revealing watercolor, John White, who had been drawing unfamiliar creatures such as flying fish and alligators, showed both operations. Since the expedition might be quickly subject to attack on reaching its destination, Grenville thought it wise to give his men experience in building a fort together; at the same time, he had them replace a pinnace lost in the storm off the Bay of Biscay: the *Tiger* needed a tender for use on shoal shores. The crew took only ten days to complete the pinnace.

While they were there, a sail on the horizon, first taken to be a Spaniard, turned out to be Cavendish in the *Elizabeth*, rejoining the flagship. She brought Grenville a welcome addition to his armed manpower, for Puerto Rico's Spanish governor at San Juan had been alerted

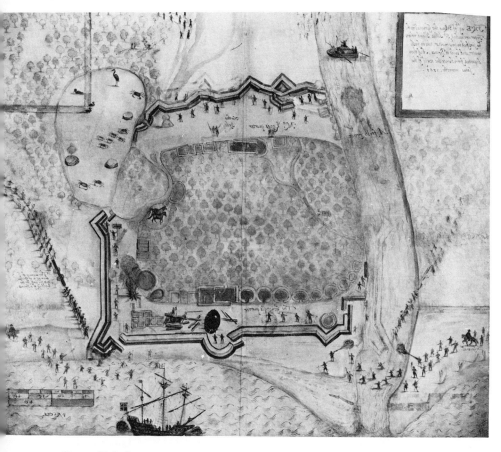

Grenville's fort on Puerto Rico, where the expedition replaced its
lost pinnace.

to his coming, and sent a detachment of forty men from San German, the town at the island's southwest corner, to keep an eye on what went on. Grenville began to engage in trade, and to capture lone ships encountered on his way.

Before they left Puerto Rico behind, an incident had revealed a clash of personalities that presaged trouble for the colony. Grenville ordered Ralph Lane to take twenty men in one of their captured frigates and go to the southern tip of the island to raid the salt pans there. Accompanied by a larger contingent than Grenville had authorized, Lane found two piles of salt ready for removal. White painted the considerable breastwork he built around the piles before loading was begun.

The sudden arrival of Spanish troops then surprised Lane. In panic, he jumped to the conclusion that the governor and all his forces were descending to annihilate him and his men. Actually, they were in all likelihood the same detachment that had watched the English before, now once more present as observers. Since they made no move to fight, Lane calmed down, loaded the rest of the salt and returned to the *Tiger*. Nothing had happened. But thereafter he nursed a great grudge against Grenville, insisting that the captain's orders had thrust him into grievous danger. When the first dispatches were sent back to London, he filed bitter complaints with Sir Francis Walsingham about the treatment he had received.

Far from being belligerent, the Spaniards at the little ports proved eager to exchange goods: Grenville began to purchase livestock and plants for the colony, and such articles as hides, sugar, and tobacco to sell once he was back in England. At Puerto de Plata on Hispaniola, he and his officers accepted an invitation to come ashore for a banquet followed by a bullfight.

On June 7 the fleet started towards the mainland and the Outer Banks. They passed the Caicos Islands. They passed the Bahamas. In Providence North Channel, they caught their first glimpse of the mainland, but did not touch on it. On June 24, finding themselves in shoal water (probably off Cape Fear) they spent the day fishing. Picking up the

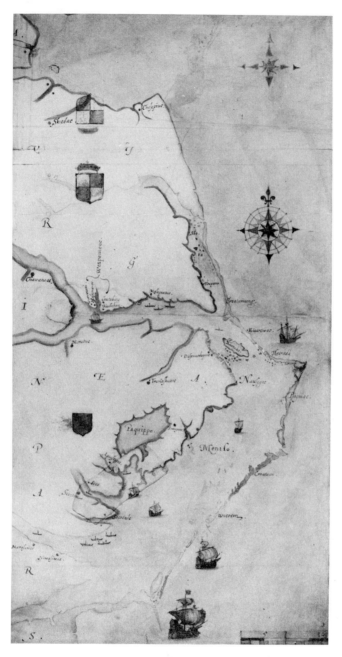

John White's map of the Outer Banks along what is now
the coast of North Carolina.

southern end of the Outer Banks, they sailed towards Cape Hatteras as far as Wococon Inlet. There, their pilot misled them.

He did not do so out of ignorance. The previous year, the reconnaisance voyagers had noticed this shallow passage into Pamlico Sound, and also identified a broader and deeper entry a few miles further north, giving it their pilot's name. This time, Fernandez did not go that far. Anchoring the *Tiger* on the ocean side of Wococon, he attempted to bring the smaller ships through the inlet into the sound. All of them grounded. With much labor and extraordinary luck, the crews floated them off uninjured. Yet in spite of this vivid warning, on the following day Fernandez attempted to sail the 200-ton *Tiger* across the shallows. Predictably, she stuck fast, and for hours lay helpless while cresting surf slammed into her, over and over. Though her back was not broken by the time she was loosened and beached, her planking had been badly wrenched, allowing salt water to pour into her hold. Everything was soaked. Since she was the only ship of any size whose location was known, the colonists were now without supplies to tide them over to their first harvest.

After staying on Pamlico Sound long enough to explore parts of it, Grenville turned north to Hatteras. On July 21, with the Indian Manteo as interpreter, he met with Granganimeo, brother of Chief Wingina of the Croatoans, to discuss placement of the colony's fort and settlement on Roanoke Island. On August 5, he sent one John Arundell home to inform the queen and Ralegh of the expedition's arrival—and urge rapid renewal of its provisions.

Three weeks later, Grenville himself weighed anchor for England, promising to be back with supplies before Easter. Luck sailed with him: seven days out, he captured the 300-ton *Santa Maria de San Vicente*. Presumably, he had left his longboat with the colonists, for he transferred to this rich prize in "a boate made with boards of chests, which fell a sunder, and sunke at the shippes side, assoone as euer hee and his men were out of it."

He stayed aboard the prize while the faster *Tiger* hastened ahead with the good news of their catch. On October 18, at Plymouth, he was "courteously received by divers of his worshipfull friends," and Ralegh was there to congratulate and thank him.

Sale of the *San Vicente*, ship and cargo, brought £50,000: the sum not only covered the entire cost of planting the colony but presented investors with a £10,000 dividend. As the sailing season closed, prospects were bright.

As soon as he was home, the Oxford scientist Harriot devoted himself to extolling what Grenville's expedition had found in his *Briefe and True Report of the New Found Land of Virginia*; Harriot's descriptions were shortly paraphrased by Michael Drayton in his poem "To a Virginia Voyage":

> You brave Heroique Minds,
> Worthy your Countries Name,
>   That Honour still pursue,
>   Goe, and subdue,
> Whilst loyt'ring Hinds
> Lurke here at home, with shame . . .
>
> And cheerfully at Sea,
> Successe you still intice,
>   To get the Pearle and Gold,
>   And ours to hold,
> Virginia,
> Earth's onely Paradise.
>
> Where Nature hath in store
> Fowle, Venison, and Fish,
>   And the fruitfull'st Soyle,
>   Without your Toyle,
> Three Harvests more,
> All greater then your Wish.
>
> And the ambitious Vine
> Crownes with his purple Masse,
>   The Cedar reaching hie
>   To kisse the Sky,
> The Cypresse, Pine,
> And use-full Sassafras . . .

Thy voyages attend,
Industrious Hakluyt,
   Whose reading shall inflame
   Men to seek fame,
And much commend
To after times thy wit.

But by the time the year 1586 opened, the colony was in straits. Grenville did not get back by Easter; it was nearer Whitsunday before he came. The final delay of his departure occurred when he grounded on his way over Bideford Bar. (The town clerk of Barnstaple, with the built-in malice of a competing town's officialdom, noted in his minute book: "16. April afore ^{sd} Sir Richard Greynvylle sailed over the bar with his flee boat and frigat but for want of suffic ^{r} water on the barr being neare upon neape he left his ship. This sir Richard Greynvylle pretended his goinge to Wyngandecora where he was last year.")

Over a three-week period that June, a series of coincidences ended Ralegh's first colony. On June 9, quite unexpectedly, Sir Francis Drake anchored off Roanoke at the head of the major fleet with which he had just scourged the chief Spanish cities of the Caribbean. His raid was the first act of open war since England's relations with Spain had been broken; his attack and Ralegh's placement of a colony were related, for an English outpost on the western Atlantic coast could be militarily useful. So Drake stopped to warn of possible reprisals and to learn how the new settlement fared. Seeing how things were, Drake offered Governor Lane and the delighted settlers a tall ship to give them mobility, and supplies to meet their urgent and so far unmet wants. But even as they talked, a sudden gale wrecked the designated ship. The colony panicked, and pressed Drake to take them all home. When he agreed, they tumbled their possessions into the longboats in such haste that all of Harriot's notes and some of White's drawings bounced overboard. By the night of June 19, Roanoke Island was empty.

Only days later, a tall ship topped the Outer Banks' eastern horizon. Ralegh, at his own expense and initiative, had sent a supply ship in

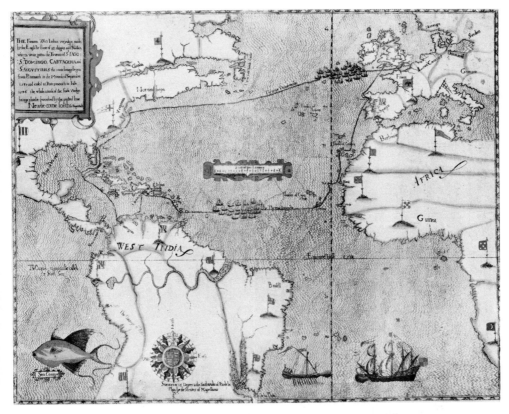

Battista Boazio's map of Sir Francis Drake's course on his 1585–86 voyage.

advance of Grenville. The captain anchored, surveyed the deserted site, and brought the supplies back to England.

Within two weeks, Grenville himself arrived with three relief vessels. He surveyed the silence, and left fifteen or eighteen men to maintain the queen's sovereignty. When he reached home, he learned that Drake had landed the evacuees at Portsmouth harbor on July 28.

He also learned that preparations to meet the long-predicted invasion were getting under way. He and Ralegh were assigned to prepare West Country coasts in case of an attempted landing there. While it was a necessary task, it was a landsman's assignment. When the Armada came, neither he nor Ralegh had a naval command.

But three years later, Grenville had his chance. In 1591, the potential capture of Philip's treasure fleet was known to afford a double measure of booty. The king had ordered the 1590 fleet to be held in Havana for fear of loss at sea through inadequate protection; now both the 1590 and the 1591 output of precious metals would be able to cross together, protected by the ships of his new building program. Lord Thomas Howard was therefore sent to the Azores in command of an English fleet of twenty-three sail. Grenville was appointed vice admiral of the expedition, and his flagship was the *Revenge*. Both the title and the ship were those that Drake had had for the Armada. At last, Grenville's opportunity to show the stuff that made him was at hand.

Toward the end of August, Howard's fleet had anchored off Flores, westernmost of the Azores. The fleet was not in fighting trim. Many of the ships had been at sea for some months, and among their crews, many men were down with the sicknesses normal after long confinement. Some vessels could not even muster strength enough to man their yards; a number were pulled up on land for rummaging, and quite a few of the sick men were temporarily set ashore.

Suddenly, a scout sailed in with startling intelligence: the Spanish fleet was not only on its way—it had arrived. The Spaniards, expected from the west, had approached from the south, masking their appearance by the elevation of the islands. Convoy and convoyed together, they numbered fifty-three sail.

A quick comparison of numbers—fifty-three Spaniards under sail against less than half that many English in the water—convinced Howard that the odds were too great to risk a fight. He ordered his ships to weigh—or even slip—their anchors and withdraw.

Withdraw? Not Grenville. He was the last to make sail—having been unwilling to leave men on shore at the mercy of the enemy—and by the time he did so the Spanish Sevillian squadron was on his weather bow. Though his master strongly advised another course, he was determined to plow his way straight through the Spanish fleet, "alleaging," as Ralegh wrote in his account of the engagement, "that he would rather choose to die, then to dishonour himselfe, his countrey, and her Majestie's shippe, perswading his companie that he would passe through the two squadrons, in despight of them, and enforce those of Sivil to give him way."

For fifteen hours thereafter, from three o'clock that afternoon until dawn the next day, the *Revenge* stood off incessant volleys and attempted boardings by Spanish men-of-war. One after another, fifteen of them attacked, from both sides. Early in the fighting, Grenville was wounded, but maintained his post until shortly before midnight. Then, as the ship's surgeon was treating his earlier wound, he was again shot, in the body and in the head; the surgeon was killed.

When day broke, Ralegh says, "All the powder of the Revenge to the last barrell was now spent, all her pikes broken, fortie of her best men slaine, and the most part of the rest hurt. In the beginning of the fight shee had but one hundreth free from sickness, and fourscore & ten sicke, laid in hold upon the Ballast. A small troop to man such a ship, & a weak garrison to resist so mighty an army."

Against Spaniards who could transfer soldiers and arms from one vessel to another, "Unto ours there remained no comfort at all, no hope, no supply either of ships, men, or weapons; the Mastes all beaten overboord, all her tackle cut asunder, her upper worke altogether rased, and in effect evened shee was with the water, but the very bottome of a ship, nothing being left over head either for fight or for defence."

By that time, Grenville, accepting the impossibility of further action, instructed his master gunner to blow the *Revenge* up, "that thereby nothing might remaine of glory or victory to the Spaniards." His gunner was willing, but his officers were not; they urged their captain to accept a composition, seeing that "there be divers sufficient and valiant men yet living, and whose wounds were not mortal, they might do their Countrey and prince acceptable service hereafter," and that the Spaniards could not make a prize of the *Revenge* because she was certain to sink. When he remained obdurate, they departed to parley on their own with the Spanish commander. They received generous terms.

Removed to the Spanish admiral's ship, Grenville died there a day or so later. Likewise a few days later, a ferocious tempest sank not only the hulk that was all that remained of the *Revenge*, but at least fourteen of the Spanish galleons, dashing them and the bodies of their crews upon the Isle of St. Michael, "to honor the buriall of that renowned ship the Revenge, not suffering her to perish alone, for the great honour achieved in her time."

Ralegh understood full well the motive for Grenville's mad defiance: "What became of the body, whether it were buried in the sea or on the land we know not: the comfort that remayneth to his friends is, that hee hath ended his life honourably in respect of the reputation wonne to his nation and countrey, and of the same to his posteritie, and that being dead he hath not outlived his owne honour."

V

The Pirate Navigator

HEN THE YOUNG FRANCIS RUSSELL, SON AND heir of the first duke of Bedford, stood godfather at the christening of the new baby in the house of a tenant on the Bedford estate near Tavistock, the child was given the sponsor's own first name. The tenant's house was in the village of Crowndale, a few miles above Plymouth; the father of the infant was a lowly yeoman, sometimes working as a shearman on the surrounding flocks, sometimes going down to the sea as a sailor, and by preference exhorting the common man as a hedgerow preacher. He and his wife lived with his elder brother, the actual operator of the farm, of which their father held the lease. His name was Edmund Drake. Young Francis Russell probably undertook the christening as one of the chores expected of families of the landed aristocracy. But a surprise was in store for the scion of the Russell family: while it was foreseeable that he should become the second duke of Bedford, it was scarcely to be imagined that the baby would grow up to be a national hero, Sir Francis Drake.

The child did not spend much of his youth on the farm. Edmund Drake's preaching was not popular with many Catholics of the area, whose adherence to the old religion was strong enough to lead them into an armed rising in 1549 when use of the new Church of England prayer book became compulsory; he also ran into trouble with the law in respect to a missing purse. Aided by his relatives the Hawkinses, he left Devon, took holy orders, and in 1560 led his expanding family—it eventually numbered twelve stout sons—to live in an abandoned hulk bogged in the mud of the Thames near the village of Upchurch in Kent, where he became vicar.

Upchurch is at the tip of the northward-projecting finger of land past which the Medway flows to its right-angle juncture with the Thames. The square church tower's distinctive shingled spire begins as a four-sided concave curve; it is topped by an octagonal cone that overhangs it like a candle-snuffer. For centuries, this spire had served mariners coming upriver as a day-guide. For the remaining seven years of his life, Edmund Drake upheld the Gospel as a life-guide to his congregation of mariners.

The surrounding area was a major shipping center, with the three closely neighboring towns of Rochester, Chatham, and Gillingham circling its base. Along the final stretch of the Medway, Queen Elizabeth's warships wintered; the garrison of the still-surviving castle that she built at Upnor at the top of the river's west bank was there to hold back intruders. Upchurch is opposite it.

Since an English clergyman's small stipend gave every incentive for prompt dispatch of children to earn their own livings, Francis, as Edmund's eldest, had been early apprenticed to a skipper who plied the coastwise trade. The man was a bachelor; he liked his apprentice so well that on his death he left the boy his boat. Francis sold the boat, and with the proceeds joined the mercantile Hawkinses in Plymouth.

Through their merchant-shipping ventures, the young man very shortly began to learn his way around the Caribbean. The trip on which he sailed in 1562, as second in command on a trading voyage to Rio de la Hacha, easternmost of the Spanish ports on the South American mainland, was uneventful enough, but in 1567, when John Hawkins took him as commander of the 50-ton *Judith* on his disastrous third slaving voyage, he shared the defeat following Spanish treachery at San Juan de Ulua on the Gulf's western shore. The rage the engagement engendered in Drake lasted his entire life.

At the conclusion of that battle, his behavior was less than exemplary. Without a word to Hawkins, he turned around and sailed for Plymouth. Understandably resentful, Hawkins—whose *Minion*, the only other English survivor, was overloaded with men and lacked food—noted that Drake's "barke the same night forsooke us in our great miserie."

The dividing line between privateering and piracy is always indistinct; in the case of Drake's next venture no attempt to draw one is necessary, for he was bent on levying a purely private war in which the

Sir Francis Drake.

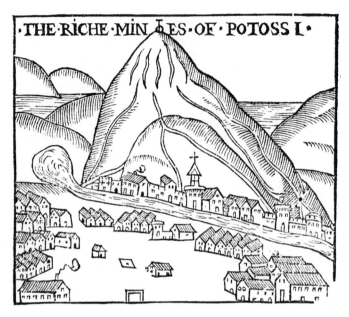

·THE·RICHE·MIN ES·OF·POTOSS I·

The Spanish silver mines at Potosi in Peru.

queen had no part. By 1570, Drake the corsair was back in the western part of the Caribbean, hiding his 25-ton *Swan* in a tiny mainland harbor surrounded by overhanging greenery into which the little ship could vanish. He was learning the route by which Philip's treasure was yearly brought from western Peru to Nombre de Dios on the eastern shore of the Isthmus, its loading point for the transfer to Seville. First, it was shipped from the Peruvian mines to the settlement of Panama on the Pacific coast. From there it came across the Isthmus either all the way by mule-train, or as far as Venta Cruces, the village at the watershed, from which, in some seasons, it could be rafted down the River Chagres to the coast and along the shore to Nombre de Dios harbor.

Having gathered this information, Drake on his third visit in 1572 brought a Hawkins ship, the 70-ton *Pasha*, as well as the *Swan*, and a crew of seventy-three, among them his younger brothers John and Joseph. Almost all were rollicking lads in their twenties, the kind who could be foreseen swaggering—or staggering—down Devon village streets with an exaggerated nautical roll to their gait as they sang interminable stanzas of such ballads as that of which two verses ran:

> For when we have received
>> Our wages for our pains,
> The Vintners and the tapsters
>> By us have golden gains.
> We call for liquor roundly,
>> And pay before we go;
> And sing, and drink,
>> Howe'er the wind doth blow . . .

> Then who would live in England
>> And nourish vice with ease,
> When he that is in poverty
>> May riches get o' th' seas?
> Let's sail unto the Indies,
>> Where golden grass doth grow;
> To sea, to sea,
>> Howe'er the wind doth blow.

Drake carried on board three knocked-down pinnaces for his men to assemble on arrival. While they were putting them together at the hideout they had used on their previous voyage, an unexpected English ship appeared and saw them. It was a moment for quick thinking—even the most casual disclosure could wreck their entire design. Drake promptly offered the captain a partnership.

In a second rapid adaptation to circumstance, Drake gave free transport back to the mainland to some Cimaroons, members of a ferocious tribe of Indians and escaped Negro slaves who lived in hatred of the Spaniards; they had been put on an island and left there to cut wood. The appreciative tribesmen became Drake's allies.

In sheer bravado, with the noisy aid of two trumpets and drums, Drake stormed Nombre de Dios by night. His entering columns, coming from different directions, effectively simulated a multitude: the few Spaniards in the town fled. In the cellar of the governor's house, the corsair and his men found bars of silver stacked as far as the beams of their lanterns carried.

Drake disdained silver; he was sure the King's Treasury building near the harbor would contain gold. But on the way there, he collapsed in a faint: early in the action, a shot had pierced his leg, and the tracks he left were edged with scarlet. After carrying him on board and binding up his wound—and pausing to relieve a departing ship of some Canary wine—the company recuperated on an island; at that point, the English captain, sure that a widespread search would shortly start, left the partnership.

Drake too expected a search, so he sailed his ships east for a feint at Cartagena. He had no intention of abandoning his project of ambushing the golden mule-train; he merely wanted to be looked for at sea while he was on land.

Returning to his hideout, Drake built a stronger base, cemented his friendship with the Cimaroons, collected victuals, and contrived to keep his boys occupied: during the rainy season, now at hand, the mule-trains did not travel. It was a disastrous interval. His brother John lost his life commanding an attempt to take a frigate with a pinnace. A pestilence (perhaps yellow fever) descended on the camp; twenty-eight of his men died of it, his brother Joseph among them. When he next moved to ambush the renewed mule-trains, he had with him eighteen Englishmen and thirty Cimaroons.

On this march, Drake's guides took him to the height of the Isthmus watershed where they showed him a tall, very ancient tree with steps cut into its trunk; from the top he looked out onto the panorama of the Pacific Ocean. William Camden, the contemporary historian and antiquary, described the moment: "After our Captain had ascended to this bower with the Chief C[i]maroon, and having, as it pleased God, at that time by reason of a breeze a very fair day, had seen that sea of which he had heard such golden reports, he besought Almighty God of his goodness to give him life and leave to sail once in an English ship in that sea." (John Oxenham, one of Drake's devoted lads on this expedition, was the first Englishman to do so; captured and turned over to the Inquisition, he was executed at Lima in 1578.)

The ambush was a fiasco. For easy identification in the moonlight, lest friend fight friend in hand-to-hand encounter, Drake's men wore white shirts. In the bushes beside the trail, they had been instructed to lie low, making no sound until called up by Drake's whistle. As they waited, a horseman came clopping by, headed west; one of the lads, having drunk much aqua vitae without any water, did not wait for the whistle; he was pulled down, but at Panama, the horseman reported the incident. As a result, the packs of the mule-train Drake ambushed contained only unimportant supplies. After exhausting his vocabulary on the culprit, Drake led his men back to the ships.

By more conventional piracy, they then collected victuals (and a pleasant windfall of gold) from passing vessels; in a captured frigate, Drake accosted a large French ship, which he found to be in great need of water. After all the deaths in his company, he needed men; again forming a partnership, he planned a new ambush on the trail, this time to take place close to Nombre de Dios. So near to safety, he thought, the cautions taken on the mountains would be relaxed or abandoned altogether. He was right, and the train proved to be 190 mules long.

After burying tons of silver in hopes of being able to come back for it, the expedition staggered towards the sea under loads of gold. A vast storm ravaged the landscape as they went. When they reached the spot on the shore where the pinnaces were to pick them up and carry them to their ships of ocean-going size, the seascape was empty. Drake was in dire need of a craft to take him to find the pinnaces, and there was none.

But there were the uprooted trees with which the storm had clogged the river; in a few hours a soggy raft with a rough-shaped mast and four oars had been hacked out of them. The storm-driven pinnaces had sheltered behind a nearby island; swiftly propelled by a remarkably favorable wind thereafter, the voyage home took only twenty-one days from the tip of Florida to Plymouth.

News of his escapade welled up from Plymouth to inundate the countryside. The nation had a storybook hero: the farm boy from Crowndale had struck gold, and captured it with reckless daring, breathtaking leadership, and apparently endless capacity for quick invention. His exploit was ready-made for balladry, and the English sang.

But only in strictest privacy could Elizabeth and her advisers join the chorus. Government policy was still to maintain ties with Philip, to whom the queen expressed her regret at her corsair's piracy, declaring her prior ignorance of his undertaking and her present ignorance of his whereabouts. (He disappeared very effectively: to this day his location is undocumented until mention of his captaincy of the *Falcon* off Ireland occurs at the end of the first earl of Essex's campaign there.)

When he reappeared in England, he was planning a new piracy, this one known to the queen and approved by Walsingham, but by Elizabeth's command kept from Burghley—she was sure he would disapprove. It was also known to Thomas Doughty, secretary to Sir Christopher Hatton, Elizabeth's Captain of the Guard, with whom Drake had struck up a friendship in Ireland.

While few, including Philip's spies, believed what they heard, Drake's preparations were purported to be for an expedition in the Mediterranean against Alexandria. His actual intent was to carry piracy to the ocean that he had seen from the very tall tree. He would get there around the tip of South America, as Ferdinand Magellan had previously done over half a century before; he would then sail past the Spanish settlements along the western South American coast and check the rumor that off the northern coast of North America there was a strait—the Strait of Anian—that led directly to the Orient. And he would take appropriate action in case he met Spanish and Portuguese carracks along the way.

Though storms delayed his actual departure from English shores until December 13, on November 2, 1577, he sailed out of Plymouth with five ships: his own 18-gun, 100-ton *Pelican*; the 16-gun, 80-ton *Elizabeth* under John Winter, son of Sir William Winter of the Navy Board; the 10-gun, 30-ton *Marygold*; the 50-ton supply-ship *Swan*, named for the ship he had taken to Nombre de Dios; and the 15-ton pinnace *Benedict*. Very shortly, the *Benedict* was forcibly exchanged at sea for a 40-ton smack whose lines Drake had found appealing; the new craft was named *Christopher* as a compliment to Hatton.

Drake had had no trouble obtaining companions: his crew included his fourteen-year-old nephew John, an artist who recorded the new and strange along their route, and his youngest brother, twenty-two-year-old Thomas. Both Thomas Doughty and his brother John were aboard also.

Their taking of ships began early. The Portuguese captain of one of them, Nuño da Silva, was an invaluable prisoner; he was familiar with the Brazilian coast. Drake kept him on board all the way to Guatulco, far up the South American west coast; his ship was renamed *Mary*. Later, da Silva put down his impressions of Drake:

Francis Drake is a man aged thirty-eight. He may be two years more or less. He is short in stature, thickset and very robust. He has a fine countenance, ruddy of complexion, and a fair beard. He has the mark of an arrow wound in his right cheek which is not apparent if one looks not with special care. In one leg he has a ball of an arquebus which was shot at him in the Indies. . . . He had seated at his table the captain, pilot and doctor. He also read the psalms and preached. . . . He carries a book in which he enters his log, and paints birds, trees and sea-lions. He is an adept in painting and carries along a boy, a relative of his, who is a great painter. When they both shut themselves up in his cabin they were always painting.

En route to La Plata, Drake and Thomas Doughty quarreled; the Doughty brothers were removed from Drake's ship to the *Christopher*. By the time the fleet reached San Julián on the lower southeastern coast of South America, Drake had become convinced that the Doughtys were plotting mutiny and practicing sorcery, and Thomas Doughty had confessed to having told Burghley of the expedition's real purposes. Bringing the entire company ashore, to serve as jurors, witnesses, and spectators, Drake tried Doughty and beheaded him at the place where Magellan had erected a gibbet long before. Some of the mariners carved themselves mugs out of wood taken from the scaffold.

Drake then offered the *Marygold* to any who wished to return to England, but found no takers. He broke up the *Swan* and the *Christopher*, having thinned his crews to man the da Silva prize. (But as they rounded the continent he likewise broke up the *Mary*; she was leaking.) Perhaps with a view to mollifying court sentiment regarding Doughty's execution, he rechristened his *Pelican*; it became the *Golden Hinde*, named for the animal that topped the crest of Sir Christopher Hatton's blazon.

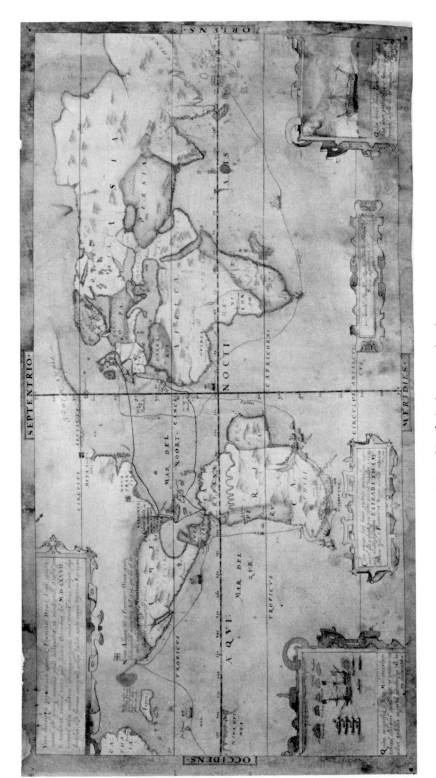

Map of Drake's circumnavigation.

Magellan's strait was now three days' sail away. Between August 20 and September 6, 1578, threading the confusing passages of the strait's twisting course, the *Golden Hinde*, the *Elizabeth*, and the *Marygold* found their way to the opening to the South Pacific. The weather there loudly belied the ocean's name: a two-week-long storm drove them pitilessly south, and the *Marygold* vanished from history. As soon as the two remaining ships had beaten their way back to a rendezvous at the strait, a second storm snapped Drake's anchor-rope, forcing him to move out to sea. The *Elizabeth*, after a three-week wait, believed him lost and returned to England.

While Drake had not the slightest intention of exploring south of the strait, that initial storm forced two new geographical facts on him and future mapmakers: the Atlantic and the Pacific joined below the Horn, and the large continent thought to lie to the southwest, Terra Australis Incognita on previous maps, had never existed.

After Drake recovered his distance and started north, the weather began to be kind. At Valparaiso, he and his men took a prize containing £8,000 in gold, a plentiful supply of wine, and a Greek pilot who knew the coast. Eight astounded Spaniards yielded her up. From the local church, Drake provided his chaplain, Francis Fletcher, with a splendid chalice and other vessels for the celebration of the Holy Communion. They then pirated their way to Callao de Lima, the port whence the year's output of precious metals from the Peruvian mines was dispatched to Panama. There, Drake learned that the great galleon *Nuestra Señora de la Concepcion* had started north only two weeks before.

The *Golden Hinde* was fast, and the winds friendly. Boarding southbound ships for news (and collecting such items as an eighty-pound gold crucifix set with emeralds) they caught up with *Nuestra Señora*. As they rounded Cape San Francisco, young John Drake, in the crow's nest, shouted that he had her in sight, and received the heavy gold chain Drake had offered to whoever should do so.

The encounter was brief; as soon as the Spaniard lost her mizzenmast to Drake's fire, she surrendered. She had a nickname, *Cacafuego* (Spitfire); a contemporary engraver used that as her label. His mislabel of the

Caca Fogo.

Caca Plata.

Drake's capture of the Portuguese merchantman *Cacafuego* in the Pacific.

Golden Hinde as the *Cacaplata* was not too wide of the mark—thereafter, her ballast consisted of silver. (But in an exchange of verbal hostilities, *Nuestra Señora*'s ship's boy, in anger and grief at the capture, resorted to the final vulgarity: she should be called "Cacafoga—yes! Cacafo!!") The loot was unbelievable—eighty pounds of gold bullion, chest on chest of coined silver, tons of silver bars, jewels, and pearls.

To an expedition consisting of a single ship, already heavily loaded, piracy began to seem redundant; Drake's plans turned to exploration of the reputed passage to India. But before starting, the *Golden Hinde* needed to be rummaged. He captured a frigate in which to keep his own cargo under guard while he beached and cleaned the *Hinde*. During the process, his pinnace took a ship arriving from China with route-wise Chinese pilots aboard; these he retained, with their charts. Once the *Hinde* was refreshed, he set off for Guatulco.

Among Drake's prisoners at this time was the Spanish captain Don Francisco de Zarate, cousin of the duke of Medina Sidonia who in 1588 was admiral of the Armada. Zarate wrote a detailed description of Drake and of ship life on board the *Golden Hinde*:

. . . His vessel is a galleon of nearly 400 tons and is a perfect sailer. She is manned with a hundred men, all of service, and of an age for warfare, and all are as practised therein as old soldiers from Italy could be. Each one takes particular pains to keep his arquebus clean. He treats them with affection, and they treat him with respect. He carried with him nine or ten cavaliers, cadets of English noblemen. These form a part of his council which he calls together for even the most trivial matter, although he takes advice from no one. But he enjoys hearing what they say and afterwards issues his orders. He has no favourite.

The aforesaid gentlemen sit at his table, as well as a Portuguese pilot, whom he brought from England, who spoke not a word during all the time I was on board. He is served on silver dishes with gold borders and gilded garlands, in which are his arms. He carries all possible dainties and perfumed waters. He said that many of these had been given him by the Queen. None of these gentlemen took a seat or covered his head before him, until he repeatedly urged him to do so. He dines and sups to the music of viols.

He carries trained carpenters and artisans, so as to be able to careen the ship at any time. Besides being new, the ship has a double lining. He also carries painters who paint for him pictures of the coast in its exact colours. This I was most grieved to see, for each thing is so naturally depicted that no one who guides himself according to these paintings can possibly go astray.

Guatulco, in Guatamala, where Drake set da Silva free, was his final stop in Spanish-occupied areas; he pressed on north for the Strait of Anian. No explanation exists of the piercing cold that he shortly reported. It was early June, and he said his rigging iced in latitude 42° north (midway up the coast of today's Oregon); at 48°, the latitude of today's Vancouver, he decided to endure no more, and turned south again. At 38°, somewhat north of today's San Francisco, he came ashore: the *Hinde* was leaking.

There commenced a ceremonial life of a kind with which Drake—who was very fond of ceremony—was unfamiliar. The Indians of the region, taking him and his men for gods, engaged in propitiatory rituals before them and eventually crowned him in feathered regalia as their ruler. He took possession of the land in the name of the queen, calling it New Albion; then, to the despair of his new subjects, he boarded the *Hinde* and sailed away.

With the Pacific in broad view and Chinese pilots to guide him, why search for what might be (and indeed was) a mythical strait? He steered southwest. Near the equator, after two months on the open sea, they began to see islands; before too long, they were in the Philippines where Magellan, caught in an intertribal war, had met his death fifty-seven years earlier. On November 3, they approached the famous Moluccas—the Spice Islands, the Oriental lands of European desire.

There, Drake enjoyed more familiar ceremony. He and the sultan exchanged gifts by longboat and canoe; the *Golden Hinde* anchored. (A map of the period contains a cartouche showing the *Hinde*, towed by four rowing canoes, being escorted to her mooring.) Canoes filled with the sultan's officers of state, all dressed in white, appeared; then came the sultan's own. Drake's guns fired a salute.

A concert, by the crew members whom Zarate had noted playing dinner music for Drake on shipboard, entranced the sultan. He promised to return the next day, and sent delicacies that evening. When not the sultan but his brother arrived on the morrow, however, Drake suspected treachery; and though his fellow officers did so, he himself did not go ashore in response to an invitation for the next evening.

No double-dealing was intended, and Drake must have regretted his decision when he heard details of the reception later. The sultan, seated on a throne and fanned by attendants, had received them in a skirt of cloth of gold, with jewels on his hands, gold chains around his neck, and a magnificent headdress. Moreover, the occasion went beyond ceremony: he offered England a commercial treaty that included a monopoly of the spice trade.

The ecstasy with which this offer would have been received by William Sanderson in London or the Hawkinses in Plymouth escaped Drake: merchandising was to him an unexplored occupation. His mind was on his route home. He went to a small island—he called it Crab Island from its wealth of crustaceans—where he gave his crew a month to build themselves up for their long journey. Soon after they sailed, however, their journey threatened to be a very short one. The *Hinde*, with her thirteen-foot draft, struck a reef and stuck fast upon it. For hours and hours she was grindingly impaled, while the crew threw off Drake's entire purchase of cloves and other valuables to lighten her. In the worst of the suspense, Francis Fletcher was heard to speculate that this catastrophe might be a judgment of the Almighty for the execution of Doughty; Drake's ever-short temper flashed, and he stretched his authority as captain to excommunicate his chaplain. But the wind changed, and the *Hinde* tilted to safety. By mid-February, they had reached Java.

The rest was easy: they rounded the Cape of Good Hope, watered at Sierra Leone, and saw no sail thereafter until they neared Plymouth. It was September 1580: they had been gone the better part of three years. Eager to test the political waters, Drake questioned a fishing smack: was the queen still alive? He did not go ashore at Plymouth; presently, he anchored in the lee of an island and sent letters of inquiry to Walsingham and Hatton. The mayor and Drake's wife Mary were rowed out to greet him there.

Elizabeth was indeed alive: for some time, the Spanish ambassador

Mendoza had been badgering her with loud complaints about her corsair's Pacific activities. Their extent was evidenced by the value of his loot, £326,580. It gave a return of £47 for each pound invested by the adventurers in the voyage. (Elizabeth herself had secretly put up £1,000.) All was very well. From his special allotment of £10,000 Drake not only financed his purchase of Buckland Abbey but a considerable number of other freeholds.

The following April 4, the first English circumnavigator was the center of ceremonies brilliant beyond his imagination. The *Golden Hinde* came to Deptford; the queen came to the *Golden Hinde*. For the sumptuous dinner served on board, she wore a new golden crown studded with emeralds and diamonds that had a familiar look about them. Reporting the celebration to his king, the Spanish ambassador described the crown: "It has five emeralds, three of them almost as large as a finger, while the two round ones are valued at twenty thousand crowns, coming as they do from Peru. He has also given the queen a diamond cross as a New Year's gift, as the custom is here, of the value of five thousand crowns." The ambassador also reported an incident that occurred upon the queen's arrival. The Seigneur de Marchmont, the representative of the Duc d'Alençon, younger brother of the French king and Elizabeth's current royal suitor, accompanied her: ". . . as she entered the Golden Hinde, her purple and gold garter slipped down and was trailing when M. de Marchaumont stooped and picked it up claiming it for his master. . . . The queen asked for it promising that he should have it back when she reached home, as she had nothing else with which to keep her stocking up. Marchaumont returned it and she put it on before him."

As a climax to the day's event, Elizabeth had ordered a knighthood to be conferred on her corsair. When the moment came for the royal tap on the shoulder of the kneeling figure, the queen handed her sword of state to Marchmont to complete the ceremony. She was a wily monarch: by this gesture, she complimented her French guest at the same time that she enabled herself to assure Philip that she did not personally do the

The tall silver-and-gilt cup, now in the Plymouth City Museum and Art
Gallery, was given by the National Art Collections Fund in 1942 in
recognition of Plymouth's part in World War II; it displays the world's
continents and oceans and the course of Drake's circumnavigation.

dubbing. Drake began to sit next to the queen at tourneys, and to dine with noble lords.

But when not aboard a ship, Drake was restless. For the next four years, no naval command could fit him into the nation's diplomatic policy. Until 1585, Elizabeth pursued her hope of peace with Spain, and Drake was the Englishman the Spaniards most resented. He spent much of his time in Devon.

He was elected Plymouth's mayor, and Bossiney in Cornwall chose him for its M.P. in the Parliament of 1584. With Frobisher, Ralegh, and others, he served on the Royal Commission on the Navy as its agenda broadened from its original mandate to investigate graft in the shipyards to consideration of naval policy and strategy for fighting ships. In 1583–84 he became an official Visitor of the Dockyards. After his first wife's death in 1583, he married an heiress, Elizabeth, daughter of Sir George Sydenham of Combe Sydenham in Somerset. But until England and Spain broke relations in 1585, Francis Drake fidgeted on the beach.

When he finally received a new command, he no longer sailed as a corsair; his reckless private piracies of the past were succeeded by royal commissions. These might be conducted with the same impudent insouciance, the same cunning seizure of an unexpected possibility as before, but he was now an accountable officer and the beat of his drum had to be timed with the national rhythm. As da Silva had observed, he was always respected and even beloved by his crews; but forever a loner, he was rarely a comfortable colleague, and he was certain to clash with an officer who wanted to fight by the book. Equals who expected to engage with him in concerted action were apt to find themselves brushed off by lightsome advice to "Follow the flagship!" given in the course of a very good dinner.

Fortunately, England's two moves into the New World in 1585, Ralegh's dispatch of a colony and Drake's attack on Spanish cities in the Caribbean, did not have to be coordinated. In the spring of 1585, when Ralegh's first settlers went to the mid-Atlantic coast of North America under Grenville, an immediate purpose was to test Spain's tolerance of so southern a location. There was considerable overlap of the boundaries of

"Virginia," the area which Elizabeth was authorizing to be named for her, and of that territory the Spaniards had long called "Florida"; the Spanish claim covered the coast from the Gulf to an indeterminate boundary well beyond Chesapeake Bay. Maintenance of a base for England's warships as far south as Roanoke Island would immensely improve English opportunities to monitor and attack Spanish treasure fleets in transit. To many on Ralegh's first expedition, this value probably outweighed any alternative usefulness that a colony might have as an economic entrepôt.

The twenty-three-ship fleet that Drake, in Her Majesty's *Elizabeth Bonadventure*, led out of Plymouth in the autumn of 1585 was more than a test; it was a deliberate provocation. Its commanders were a distinguished company: Vice Admiral Frobisher in the *Primrose*; Rear Admiral Francis Knollys, the queen's relative, in the galleon *Leicester*; Edward Winter in Her Majesty's *Aid*; General Christopher Carleill, Walsingham's son-in-law, in the *Tiger*. The younger generation included Drake's brother Thomas and John Hawkins's son Richard.

Once in the familiar waters of the Caribbean, after an initial stop to burn Santiago and other towns in the Cape Verde Islands, Drake the naval commander behaved very much like Drake the pirate. When he took Santo Domingo on Hispaniola, oldest and most splendid of the Spanish cities, dispatches to Seville reported: "Unless provided, these people are so terrorized, poor, and defenseless that they will abandon the country." When he took Cartagena, the current capital of the Spanish Main, dispatches to Seville made no distinction between officer and pirate: "The damage done by this corsair amounts to more than 400,000 ducats . . . in burning and looting it the English have left this city so completely destroyed and desolate that its present condition deserves the deepest pity." As planned in advance, his next move was to be a double capture: occupation of Nombre de Dios on the east side of the Isthmus and Panama on the west side would achieve a clear-cut severance of the lines of communication between the Peruvian sources of Spain's treasure and the fleets conveying it to Spain.

But here, Drake the naval commander took over. The last time he had been here, he was in his early thirties, free-lancing with a group of youngsters out on the town. But now, mid-fortyish and responsible for a royal command, he had second thoughts. Disease had twice stricken the soldiery under him: the first infection, probably yellow fever, had killed over 200 in eighteen days; the second, doubtless malaria, was slower-acting but no less deadly. If he sent home for reinforcements, he might be able to hold Cartagena. But what would such withdrawals mean in case an invasion of England were becoming more likely, and how long would additional troops take to get over to him? Uncharacteristically, he decided against further adventure. On the way home in early 1586 he paused to ravage St. Augustine; in June, he stopped at Ralegh's Roanoke, and took the colony with him.

The English populace might cheer Drake as a returning hero all over again, but the Privy Council minuted that this voyage did not have "so good success as had been hoped." Drake had carried with him a schedule of ransoms he hoped to extract from cities and individuals; the actual yields, from both mayors and merchants, were discouraging, and though he brought back valuable ordnance, his finds of treasure were scanty. Investors in the voyage received only 15/- for each pound subscribed.

Early the next year, however, Drake was given a command of the kind he had long coveted: Philip's Armada was taking shape rapidly in his ports, and Drake was authorized to disrupt preparations there. Elizabeth supplied him with four navy ships, the *Elizabeth Bonadventure*, the *Dreadnought*, the *Rainbow*, and the *Golden Lion*; the Lord High Admiral sent the *White Lion*, and various companies, towns, and Drake himself supplied other vessels for a very imposing fleet. He sailed for Cadiz.

His vice admiral, on the *Golden Lion*, was William Borough, Clerk of the Ships at the Navy Board. Borough's family were good Devonians and mariners; their ancestral home was outside the village of Northam near Appledore on the peninsula between the Torridge estuary and Barnstaple Bay, at the first place within the bar where ships could lie up. No one could impugn either his courage or his seamanship: under his elder brother Stephen, master of the *Edward Bonadventure* in Richard Chancellor's northeastern explorations of the 1550s, William had dared the unknown Arctic ice as a common mariner. (Charles Kingsley used him as his model for Amyas Leigh in *Westward Ho!*) But he was a very careful man, mindful of protocol and insistent on sailing by the book.

To Borough's horror, Drake, though unfamiliar with Cadiz harbor, sailed straight into it, without even holding a council of his officers in advance. The raid was a phenomenal success, and therefore might have been forgiven: no English ship grounded; the destruction of shipping and stores was awesome. But when it was over, Drake did not depart. He had heard a rumor that the 1,500-ton flagship of Spain's Lord High Admiral lay deeper in the harbor. He anchored where he was until morning, then moved into the inner pool to sack and sink her, crowning success with this final coup. The score was thirty-three Spanish ships and two galleys sunk, and four more taken away as victuallers.

But when Drake expected to leave, the wind died, and the fleet lay under fire in the outer harbor for some hours, helpless as a raft of sitting ducks. Borough, without permission, managed to work his way out.

Drake's next objective was Lisbon—while that harbor was too well fortified for entry, shipping could be picked up as it came and went. But first, he needed to repair and water. At Cape St. Vincent, he entered the little bay and fought side-by-side with his men as they climbed the overhanging height and took the castle of Sagres above it.

The landing was known to be forbidden by the orders given to Drake; this transgression proved to be the last straw in the worsening of relations between him and his vice admiral. Borough had begun the break by sending over to the flagship a letter complaining of Drake's failure to follow proper procedure with his officers, especially with him; this initial exhibition of stuffiness appears to have been followed by others, and his pull-out at Cadiz could be called desertion, if also common sense. The crew of the *Golden Lion* then mutinied and sailed home with their commander. Drake eased his feelings by condemning the lot of them to death in absentia.

Borough would have been further exasperated had he stayed, for Drake suddenly vanished. Once again, he had heard a rumor: the carrack

San Felipe, homing from the Orient, was said to be at the Azores, and he was off to test the rumor's reality. Possibly the largest merchantman in any navy, this ship had been claimed by Philip as a personal prize when he occupied Portugal. Drake found her, took her, transferred her crew and passengers to another ship, put a prize crew of his own aboard, and sailed for Plymouth. Her fabulous cargo brought £114,000; Burghley received £1,000 for distributing the profit among the shareholders, and Drake, feeling every inch a pirate again, walked away with £17,000.

But the sober evidence brought home from Cadiz was irrefutable: Philip's Armada would very soon set sail. Basic plans for England's defense were completed and ships allocated to commanders. Drake, and others advocating offense as the best defense, recommended further strikes to destroy or disable the Spanish in their home ports; in late May 1588, a fleet started towards Finisterre but was storm-driven home again. Elizabeth then forbade another such voyage: if her ships missed contact with an invading fleet on its way, the English coast would lie open and undefended.

Under the defensive plan now agreed on, two concentrations of the ships Hawkins had made ready would be stationed at the nation's two strategic entrances: one to guard the Channel's western end, and one to protect the east coast from Parma's army. The allotment of commands went by protocol; Drake's attempt to head the western squadron, on the strength of being the Admiral of Devon, did not consort with it. Elizabeth's Lord High Admiral was head of the fleet, and regardless of relative naval competence, he was the suitable person to be visibly in charge when the Spanish appeared. (It was equally suitable for his nephew to deputize for him as head of the eastern squadron.) Below them, rank should and would be awarded to the top professional specialists.

Accordingly, Charles, Lord Howard of Effingham, appeared off Plymouth on May 23, with a force that included eighteen royal ships. For the impressive arrival ceremony, Drake, flying his flag as Devon's admiral, led out the vessels already on station, and lowered his standard in salute. Howard, flying the royal standard, his own flag as Lord High Admiral, and a flag signifying Vice Admiral of the Fleet, acknowledged

Drake's response. He then ordered the vice admiral's flag to be lowered from the flagship and presented, henceforth to be flown by Drake. The chain of command thus established represented both the hierarchical structure of English society and the height of nautical skill.

Equally balanced was the council of war set up by Howard. Besides himself, its members were Vice Admiral Sir Francis Drake; Lord Thomas Howard, second son of the duke of Norfolk, Thomas Howard III; Lord Edmund Sheffield, who had served in the Netherlands under Leicester; Sir Roger Williams, a professional soldier with a long record of Continental campaigns; and three exceptional sea-captains: John Hawkins, newly named Rear Admiral of the Fleet; Martin Frobisher; and Thomas Fenner. When Captain John Fleming brought the news that the Armada had been sighted, its reception committee was in place.

VI

The Running of the Armada

OR TEN DAYS AFTER THE TALL SHIPS OF SPAIN'S great fleet swept into view off Plymouth Hoe on July 20, tension among the English mounted. Sometimes as eyewitnesses along the coast, more often as listeners to rumors spread at the bars of local taverns by fishermen who had caught glimpses of the action, Englishmen heard how, day by day, Philip's navy, in seemingly inexorable advance, was moving up the Channel. Past Plymouth. Past Portland Bill. Past the Isle of Wight. Into the strait, only twenty-two miles wide, that separates Calais and Dover. Just beyond, off Dunkirk, union with Parma's army was scheduled to begin the ferrying of foreign invaders to the English shore.

And as public misgivings circulated by word of mouth, little pinnaces, dispatched by English commanders to officials on shore, kept landing with more accurate but no less disquieting versions of enemy progress.

Watchers on the Hoe at Plymouth had quickly compared the Armada's seemingly unbelievable numbers with Drake's twenty-three-ship fleet that had appeared so overwhelming when he led it out of their port for his raids on the cities of the Spanish Main three years before. All told, Philip's Armada contained some 130 vessels, with its victuallers, transports, and smaller ships sheltered behind a rim of high-castled galleons and converted merchantmen. The galleon was Spain's standard fighting ship, longer and narrower than her average merchantman and therefore more manageable; in addition, this fleet contained four of the newly developed galleasses, warships that could be either rowed or sailed and were therefore movable independent of the wind. The Armada's wedge-shaped order of battle forced an attacking fleet to choose between meeting its frontal squadrons head on and approaching the tips from the rear, where some of the most formidable ships were stationed in readiness.

The track of the English ships as they worked their way out of Plymouth
and took up positions west of the Armada.

The Spanish decks were crowded with fighting men: aboard the
warships, military companies far outnumbered mariners. Spanish strategy for naval combat, little altered since the placement of heavy artillery
below decks, still envisaged a grapple with the opponent, a hurried
clamber into his ship, and a hand-to-hand fight on the crowded and
slippery deck. Once a boarding had been completed, the struggle—
though more compact—differed little from a land engagement.

The strategy carried with it an important implication. The ranking
commanders on the Spanish ships were military men. From the point of
view of the soldiers, the seamen were essentially their servants, whose

job was to transport fighting units to locations at which they could engage. The military contingents on board would be held responsible for the results of an encounter at sea, exactly as they would be if the clash had occurred on land. They therefore outranked as well as outnumbered the crews whose purpose was to position them. Friction between the two was normal.

Philip's original selection for command of his Enterprise had been Don Alvaro de Bazán, marquis of Santa Cruz, a vigorous and experienced veteran of sea battles, including the critically important defeat of the Turks at Lepanto a few years before; and the original date the king had set for the departure of the fleet was the autumn of 1587. But preparations had been slow, and Drake's destructive raid on Cadiz had slowed them further. Increasingly discontented with the tempo, Philip ordered that ready or not, the expedition was to sail on February 15, 1588. But a week before that date, Santa Cruz died.

As replacement, Philip named the thirty-seven-year-old Alonzo Perez de Guzmán el Bueno, duke of Medina Sidonia. The town from which the family derived its ducal title is in the far south, in Andalusia close to Cadiz, but the palace that had been the family residence since the thirteenth century and remains so today, is close to the port of Sanlúcar, on the estuary where the Guadalquivir River completes its course from Seville to the sea. The duke was a grandee of national prestige, a person who would receive respect from commanders from all of Spain's varied regions. But he was not a navigator—on ocean voyages he was a consistent victim of seasickness—and he protested to the king that he lacked experience and skill to command so large a force. When Philip's purpose remained fixed, this new Captain General for the Ocean Seas, in his great flagship, the *San Martin*, simply had to accept and do as best he could. Loyally and gallantly, that was what he did.

On April 25, 1588, at the altar of Lisbon's ornately magnificent cathedral on the height above the Tagus harbor, the archbishop of Portugal celebrated a high mass with the Cardinal Archduke, Philip's viceroy of Portugal, in attendance. The great flag that was to be the Armada's standard, after blessing at the altar, was presented to Medina Sidonia.

The port city of Lisbon, from which the Armada set sail.

The figures on it symbolized Philip's perennial equation of his royal purposes with the Will of God; the royal arms were at its center, with the figures of Christ and His Holy Mother occupying the positions that the language of heraldry designates as supporters. The battle-cry below them read: *Exurge, domine, et vindica causam tuam* ("Rise up, O Lord, and vindicate thy cause"). The service concluded, a bearer on a white horse paraded the standard to the populace as the solemn procession filed down into the harbor under this sign.

(The grandees of Lisbon had not been invited to this ceremony on the ground of lack of room; the omission may also have been in recognition of a certain lack of enthusiasm in the country that Philip had occupied by force only eight years before. After all, Medina Sidonia's flagship was appropriated Portuguese property. And a two-week wait for a favorable wind—it did not come until May 11—was required before the relieved city could watch the fleet go.)

Spain's European dominions had all sent ships and men. A Babel of languages rippled along the wharves as the ships' boats filled: besides the various provinces of Spain and Portugal, crews hailed from Venice, Ragusa, Genoa, Sicily, the Basque country, and Florence.

When the ships formed up, with Medina Sidonia in the *San Martin* was his chief of staff, Don Diego Flores de Valdes, commander from Castile. His vice admiral, Juan Martinez de Recalde, was in the great galleon of the Biscayans, the *San Juan de Portugal*. The forward center of the wedge contained two squadrons of ten galleons each, one from Portugal and the other from Castile, four greatships (converted merchantmen) from the West Indian trade, and four galleasses from Naples, commanded by Hugo de Moncada. Next, flanking these, came four squadrons of ten merchantmen each; among their leaders were Miguel de Oquendo of the Guipúzcoans on the Gulf of Gascony, Pedro de Valdes of the Andalusians, and Martin de Bertendona of the Italian Levanters. (Don Pedro and Diego de Valdes were cousins, but devoted enemies.)

Among the armed merchantmen was the huge *Florencia*, largest of all the ships that sailed from Spain and exceeded only by Elizabeth's *Triumph*. By rights, she was the property of the grand duke of Tuscany. That dignitary was one of Philip's nominal allies, but was currently outraged: the *Florencia* was his only galleon, and she had been snatched in Lisbon harbor when he sent her there on a purely commercial errand.

In addition to the fighting ships, there were thirty-four zabras, frigates, and pataches (scouts and fast-moving freighters), twenty-three urcas (the slower, Baltic-type freighters), and four Portuguese row-galleys, normally used only in calmer waters.

By contrast to the Spaniards, the English had some years earlier begun to build lighter—and far more maneuverable—vessels to be used as weapons in themselves. The *Triumph* and a few others of Elizabeth's older ships were as large and as high-charged as the Spanish vessels, but in general, ships of 200–500 tons had become the preferred English size, and were treated essentially as gun-carriages that could quickly be turned about to fire their cannon in alternate broadsides, forcing their opponents to yield by dismasting their sails or penetrating their hulls, often below the waterline, from a considerable distance. Such a plan of action made boarding unnecessary, and reduction of the military complement not only decreased the ratio of soldiers to seamen but materially lessened the problem of victualling. More significantly, it initiated a transfer of power and prestige from the military commander to the

The *Ark Royal*, Lord Howard of Effingham's flagship.

admiral. Drake's demand a decade earlier, that in times of crises, "I must have the gentleman to pull with the mariner, and the mariner with the gentleman," would never have been heard on a Spanish galleon.

Of the fifty-four ships at Plymouth, Howard's flagship was the *Ark Royal*, commissioned by Sir Walter Ralegh as the *Ark Ralegh* over a year before, and bought and renamed by the queen while still on the stocks. Howard was entranced with her; he wrote Burghley: "I pray you tell her Majesty from me that her money was well given for the 'Ark Raleigh'—for I think her the odd ship in all the world for all conditions . . . We can see no sail great or small but how far soever they are we fetch them and speak with them."

The *Ark* was an 800-ton four-master. She had a spritsail at the bow; her fore-, main-, and mizzenmasts were square-rigged, with topsails and topgallant sails above; a lateen sail with a topsail aided steering on her bonadventure. The forecastle and sterncastle were modestly low, in accordance with the new ship design approved by both Ralegh and Hawkins.

As pictured in the engraving of the ship reprinted here, her open ports on her lower decks and on the covered portions of her orlop show her capable of a twenty-three-gun broadside; four more cannon flank her rudder and one surmounts the captain's walk on her stern.

On the fore and the bonadventure masts, she flies St. Georges, with their red crosses on white grounds; the royal standard is on the main, and a standard with a large Tudor rose on the mizzen. Streaming from the foremast are two bifurcated pennants, the upper showing a rampant lion, the lower, an anchor. A pennant flying from the tip of the bowsprit carries a cross on a striped ground alternating the green and white of the Tudor colors. The crow's nest of the mainmast tethers a still larger striped pennant—the Elizabethans were partial to such decoration. On the open deck, a large banner, square as all flags then were, displays royal quarterings.

The decks are full, and the rigging and crow's nest are alive with busy mariners. At the top of the poop, a stern lantern prepares the ship to guide the fleet after dark. In the upper left-hand corner of the engraving, a brisk and favorable wind, blown by an allegorical figurehead protruding from a cloud, propels the ship forward: only the foresail and the topsail on the mainmast are unfurled to catch it.

Lord Thomas Howard was in the 600-ton *Golden Lion*, an old ship, but just now rebuilt. Vice Admiral Drake commanded the 500-ton *Revenge*; Rear Admiral Hawkins, the 800-ton *Victory*; his son Richard had the 360-ton *Swallow*. The *Revenge* was the prototype of the new class of fighting ship; the *Victory*, though one of the older vessels in the fleet, had been recently rebuilt. Martin Frobisher, in the 1,100-ton *Triumph*, captained both the oldest and the largest ship of all. Many of the lesser craft in the western squadron were armed merchantmen; a few were volunteered privateers.

On the two sides, these were the human contestants in the forthcoming trial. But a third force, well able to determine what each side could do, was actively engaged, alternately aiding and obstructing the Spanish and the English purposes. Both fleets, since they were composed of sailing ships, were unavoidably and irresistibly dependent on a sequence of unpredictable winds upon the waters. "Fleets at sea," the Holy Roman Emperor Charles V had once remarked to his son Philip, "are subject to as great uncertainties as the waves that bear them." After the battle, the design on the reverse of an English medal carried a comparable note of realism: "God blew with his wind, and they scattered."

When a fleet had the weather gauge of its opponent, when, that is, the wind was at its back, its commander could determine the course of the day's action. By contrast, a fleet with a head wind against it could do no more than tack out of the way if it had enough space to do so, or else await either the onslaught of the adversary or the humiliation of grounding on a lee shore. When the wind died, ships had to drift becalmed on whatever current moved, though in a worst case, they could lower their longboats and try to warp or tow themselves out of danger.

Captains in both fleets were convinced that God was on their side. The English sang a solemn prayer:

> From mercilesse invaders,
>> From wicked men's device,
> O God! arise and helpe us,
>> To quele owre enemies.
>
> Sinke deepe their potent navies,
>> Their strength and corage breake,
> O God! arise and arm us,
>> For Jesus Christ, his sake.

The Spaniards had been led confidently to expect a miracle. But as they made their way up the Channel, nature, at least, proved fickle. On arrival, they had the wind with them, but later on, around-the-compass changes tested the seamanship of all commanders.

SATURDAY, JULY 20: NIGHT DECISION

A landlubber might applaud as an instance of daredevil bravado the legend that when the Armada came in sight on July 20 Francis Drake contemptuously remarked to the companions with whom he was bowling on Plymouth Hoe: "We have time enough to finish the game and beat the Spaniard too!" Actually, the players knew that they did indeed have time on their hands, and that because of it, their ships were in a very dangerous situation: caught in harbor with both wind and tide inbound. At this point, the Armada could have bottled up half the English fleet, for not until ten o'clock that night would the ebb tide be strong enough to help Elizabeth's ships tow or warp their way out to sea against the wind under cover of darkness. Half of England's heavy firepower was in jeopardy.

Somehow or other, they got out. But before doing so, the captains had to make a daring and definitive decision. Their mission was to prevent the Spaniards from landing on English soil or joining Parma's forces. If their squadron did not disrupt the Armada as it proceeded up the Channel, any substantial English hindrance would have to depend on action by the navy's other concentration near the Strait of Dover. Yet if they came out to the east of Philip's fleet, tacking their way against the wind, the Spanish ships, enjoying the weather gauge, could choose their points of attack or drive them ignominiously before them. The alternative on which Howard and Drake decided was to fall in behind the invaders. They would thereby gain the weather gauge, but the best they could do with it was to harass the Armada's progress from a following position.

SUNDAY, JULY 21: FIRST ENGAGEMENT

Next morning the English, coming from the rear, mounted a long-range cannonade on the northern tip of the wedge. After observing the distance at which the English intended to fight, Spain's Vice Admiral

Recalde, commanding the *San Juan de Portugal*, baited a trap for them. Sending the rest of his squadron forward, he tempted his pursuers to attack an apparently abandoned galleon. If they did so, and others of both sides joined in, a general melee would permit the boarding tactics that were a Spanish specialty.

Drake, Hawkins, and Frobisher approached, but only close enough for their guns to batter the *San Juan*. After about an hour, Recalde's squadron returned with Medina Sidonia and shepherded the *San Juan* back into the fleet, where the damage she had sustained could be worked on.

That first day, the commanders were warily sizing each other up. Both were impressed. Medina Sidonia's log observed, "Their ships are so fast and so nimble they can do anything they like with them." Drake wrote Lord Henry Seymour in the eastern squadron, "They are determined to sell their lives with blows." Lord Howard sent ashore for more men and ships.

Following the engagement, however, the Spanish suffered accidents to two of their capital ships. In a collision, Don Pedro de Valdes's flagship, *Nuestra Señora del Rosario*, lost her bowsprit and foremast. The *San Martin* put a line on her to take her in tow, but a choppy sea snapped it and rising wind prevented attachment of a replacement; she had to be left drifting.

In a second disaster, gunpowder stored astern on Miguel de Oquendo's *San Salvador* suddenly blew up, maiming and burning many of the crew. (Stories that malicious insubordination caused the accident sped over Europe in multiple versions—in all of them the powder had been intentionally ignited by a malcontent, but the nationality of that individual varied with the place where the tale was told.) Next day, the ship began to sink; two days later, after partial unloading, she was abandoned. The Captain Fleming who had first sighted the Spanish fleet promptly towed her to Weymouth as a prize; observers smilingly recalled his lucrative past as a pirate.

The explosion on the *San Salvador*.

DETAIL: Bottom left center.

MONDAY, JULY 22: DRAKE'S DISAPPEARANCE

During the night of July 21–22, Howard was exposed to serious danger caused by his own vice admiral. In permitting Drake to lead the fleet's advance, Howard had ordered the other ships to be guided by his stern light. After some hours, Drake doused this light and disappeared. Howard, with only two ships in close company, peered into the darkness for a time, then sighted a lantern and followed it. But by the light of first dawn he saw, to his horror, that this lantern was actually on Medina Sidonia's poop: the *Ark Royal*, the *Mary Rose*, and the *Bear* had almost joined the Armada. There is no English record of how they got away; a single Spanish account reports that Hugo de Moncada asked permission to attack with his galleasses but for some ungiven reason was refused.

The first part of the story Drake told on rejoining the fleet that afternoon was less than convincing: he said that seeing unidentified shapes upon the water, he had pursued them until they turned out to be harmless German merchantmen; he then left the chase. The reckless risk he had caused was well worthy of a court-martial. Yet his return was accepted without complaint because of the rest of his account, even though it sounded more like Drake the pirate than Drake the vice admiral. His nose for a prize had led him to the drifting *Rosario*, and he now held her captain, Don Pedro de Valdes, awaiting Howard's pleasure in his cabin on the *Revenge*. The *Rosario* herself was on her way to Torbay under Jacob Whiddon, captain of Ralegh's *Roebuck*. Her yield, the most lucrative of the entire campaign, was forty-six great guns, other arms and ammunition, and 55,000 ducats of gold in her strongbox.

TUESDAY, JULY 23: SECOND ENCOUNTER

As the Armada approached Portland Bill, the wind shifted, blowing briskly from the east. Medina Sidonia, now possessing the weather gauge, turned on his pursuers and fought an engagement at considerably closer range than its predecessor, amid an almost incessant exchange of cannonades.

Drake's capture of the *Rosario*.

DETAIL: Bottom left.

Seeing Frobisher apparently in trouble, becalmed close to shore, Howard profited by a further shift of wind to relieve him. Frobisher may not have wanted aid; he may have been engaged in a ruse to entice enemy ships towards him from the east. Their direct route, close to Portland Bill, would have grounded them on a shallow bar called The Shambles, along which the tide raced in tricky currents. Philip had foreseen such possibilities, ordering each of his squadrons to have with it one or more pilots—Dutch, renegade English, or the like—familiar with obstructions along the English coast. But in any case Howard's appearance warded off the *Triumph's* danger.

The same shift of wind left Spain's Vice Admiral Recalde exposed in his repaired *San Juan de Portugal* on the southern tip of the wedge; Medina Sidonia, sending other ships to the rescue, stood alone to take a battering of broadsides.

At the end of the day, results were inconclusive. Again the Armada continued its forward progress, and again Howard sent urgent messages ashore: he would absolutely have to have more powder and shot if his ships were to continue to fight as intensively as they had done on this day's engagement.

WEDNESDAY, JULY 24: EASTWARD DRIFT

After the engagement near Portland Bill, the fleets—doubled by their reflections in still waters—drifted in calms and light western airs. Medina Sidonia dispatched small ships with messages to Parma, urging him to send specific plans for their meeting at once. He got none in reply, for though Parma believed that conquest of England was necessary, in earlier dispatches to Philip he had disapproved of the king's current attempt, and his correspondence continued to be with the king rather than with the king's approaching commander. The previous autumn, at the time of the original schedule for the invasion, Parma had had his army at the peak of readiness. But after the postponement, while diplomatic negotiations with England were drawn out to cover the gap, a wet and cold Flanders winter had sickened and diminished his forces, and he was having his own serious troubles getting delivery of enough shallow-draft Dutch boats to tow his men, horses, and supplies out into water deep enough for the Armada to join up and commence convoy. The Armada's galleons drew twenty-five to thirty feet, far too much for entry into any Netherlands port except English-held Flushing and Brill, and in any case Parma's troops were further south on the Nieuport-Dunkirk coast. The only barges he could obtain were flat-bottomed cattle boats normally used on Dutch canals, without sails, movable only as tows. His supply of fly-boats—the fast sailers of Dutch design in which Justin of Nassau, the Dutch stadtholder, patrolled the Netherlands coast—was miserably small, only about a dozen where fifty would have been inadequate. Since the gap between his army and Medina Sidonia's fleet was currently unbridgeable, Parma had no plans to suggest.

A minor battle during the morning of July 24 revolved around the *Gran Griffon*, flagship of the urcas, which had straggled; once more the fighting was at closer range than previously, and caused larger casualties in both fleets. That afternoon, the English reorganized their ships in four squadrons, commanded by Howard, Drake, Hawkins, and Frobisher. Later, a breeze sprang up in the west, and over the night of July 24–25 the fleets approached the Isle of Wight. Once again, Howard worried lest Medina Sidonia attempt a landing.

THURSDAY, JULY 25: OFF THE ISLE OF WIGHT

Next morning, the sea was dead calm; Hawkins ordered his ships to be towed by their longboats into fighting positions near two slightly damaged stragglers, the galleon *San Luis de Portugal* and the West Indian merchantman *Santa Ana*. Howard brought his *Ark*, and Lord Thomas his *Lion*. But three of the Spanish galleasses, rowing at speed and towing Don Alonso de Leiva's great carrack, *La Rata Coronado*, into position to cover their action, drew the stragglers back into the crescent. Medina Sidonia observed what appeared to be an opportunity: Frobisher was again immobilized inshore. But Frobisher got out his rowers, and other English ships sent longboats to supplement them; the wind freshened,

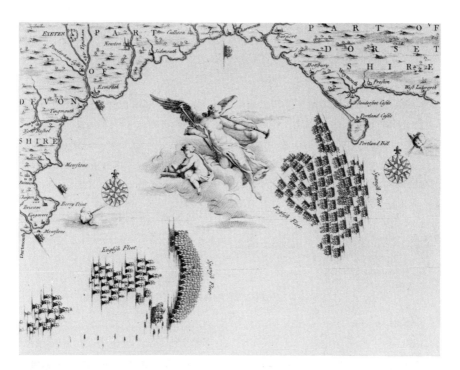

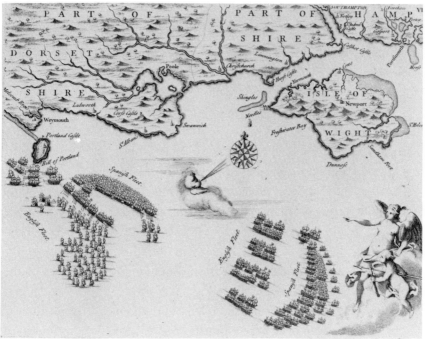

The fleets off Portland Bill and the Isle of Wight.

the *Triumph*'s drooping sails bulged, and the commander rejoined his squadron.

At the same time, Drake attacked the Spanish starboard wing. He had two motives: it might be possible to cut another prize away from the formation, and his impact would in any case jostle the Spanish line towards the northeast. There lay The Owers, a bank of shoal water and occasional rock of whose existence there was a chance that the Spaniards might be unaware. The ruse almost worked; but the *San Martin*'s pilot saw fawn-colored water alongside and a quick command swung the fleet's northern tip south-southeast to safety.

FRIDAY, JULY 26: WORRIED COMMANDERS

On Friday the twenty-sixth, both commanders took stock. In a fine gesture, as if there had been a victory, Howard knighted Hawkins, Frobisher, and others. But in fact, he was almost out of ammunition, and the Armada, after a week and four successive engagements since it was sighted west of Plymouth, was still proceeding in good order in its chosen direction. He called out the east-coast squadron, and reiterated to those on shore that somewhere, somehow, and fast, powder and cannon-balls must be found for his resupply.

Meanwhile, the Spaniards were more and more troubled about the rendezvous. Medina Sidonia knew that beyond the Calais-Dover strait there was no friendly or neutral port of sufficient depth to receive him. Unless he and Parma united, his voyage—the entire Enterprise of England—would fail, and he had had no word. He had written the king that, not having heard from Parma, "I can only proceed slowly to the Isle of Wight, and go no further until he informs me of the state of his forces. All along the coast of Flanders there is no harbour to shelter our ships, and if I took the armada from the Isle of Wight it might be driven on the shoals, where it would certainly be lost. To avoid such an obvious danger, I have decided to stay off the Isle of Wight until I know what the duke is doing, as the plan is that the moment I arrive he should come out with his fleet, without making me wait a minute . . ." But by this time he was beyond the Isle of Wight, and a shift of wind to the northwest was even now pushing him towards the shoals of the French shore. His only choice seemed a miserable option: to anchor in the sands that front the chalk cliffs of Calais Roads until a definite meeting could be concerted.

SATURDAY, JULY 27: THE SPANISH AT ANCHOR

So on Saturday afternoon, the Armada's cables slipped out, and one by one, the great Spanish ships lay immobilized at anchor. To the windward of them, only the length of a cannon shot away, the complete English fleet—for Howard had now been joined by Seymour's squadron—encircled them like a wolf-pack closing in on its quarry.

SUNDAY, JULY 28: THE NIGHT OF THE FIRESHIPS

Both captains general were well familiar with the classic action appropriate for a windward fleet facing an enemy backed up against a lee shore: loose fireships to float among the anchored hulls. Rudders fixed and all sails set, dipping eerily with wind and tide, spewing flames and burning fragments in all directions, these monsters would sidle into the immobilized enemy fleet. A spring (semi-monthly) high tide and a south wind furthered the English purpose.

Lest opportunity be lost through the time it would take to bring more expendable craft out from the English shore, Howard's captains volunteered valuable shipping. Drake sacrificed a 200-tonner, his own *Thomas of Plymouth*, and Hawkins matched him; these and six other stout ships, tonnages from 90 to 200, were combined in a close-moving pyre. When the heat reached its height, their loaded guns would explode, sending up showers of red-hot metal.

The fireships' advance broke all semblance of Spanish order. The Spanish soldiers and sailors thought the monsters might be some of the "hell-burners" used against Parma's forces at the siege of Antwerp. They had heard grisly horror-stories about such giant bombs, capable of emitting a mile-wide swath of flaming destruction, and the likelihood

Fireships launched against the anchored Spanish fleet.

DETAIL: Center.

that they were now being used was enhanced by the rumor that their inventor, the Italian engineer Giambelli, was currently in England, which was in fact the case.

Cutting cables, the Armada clawed itself out in formless disarray in wind that was strong and rising. Before long, it had reached gale force, and was pushing all ships north through the Strait of Dover.

MONDAY, JULY 29: THE BATTLE OF GRAVELINES

The next morning, the greatest engagement of the Armada campaign shattered the silence off the town of Gravelines on the French coast south of Dunkirk. Eventually, both fleets were fully involved. But before all forces had entered the melee, Howard's squadron was held back for a looting expedition as extraneous to the matter at hand as Drake's pursuit of the *Rosario*. The rudder of Moncada's *San Lorenzo* had required repair as the Armada first entered the Channel; now it had been ripped off and lost, tangled in a neighbor's cable during the escape from the fireships. Without power to steer, the ship went aground before Calais.

Howard's *Ark* was far too deep-draft to pursue, but the admiral sent his longboats to board her, and after a ball killed Moncada the *San Lorenzo*'s crew and galley slaves (she was a galleasse) scrambled for shore on her lee side, as the English pulled themselves up over a port side high out of water. She was indeed a major ship, but quite unable to move, and until the looting was over, Howard's entire squadron was out of action.

The major engagement had begun at first light; it lasted all day. Against everything that Medina Sidonia could assemble, all of England's royal ships, all of her armed merchantmen, all of her privately owned privateers, and some five score of smaller vessels took part. Both sides were using their last reserves of ammunition. (Both sides were also very short of food and water.) Yet Spanish discipline had brought the Armada again into combat order. Each side was fighting at the top pitch of its courage and skill.

The English had by this time realized that the previously shortened distances from which they were shelling were still too great for maxi-

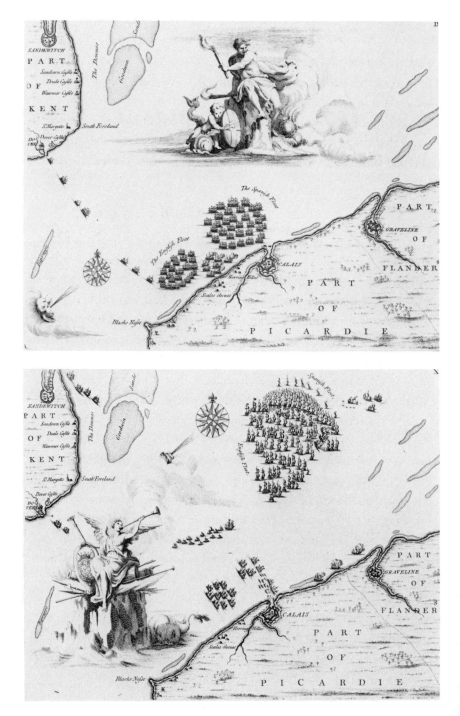

The battle of Gravelines.

mum results from their guns; on this day they moved much nearer their targets, and Spanish shortages of shot gave them partial immunity from retaliation as they closed. Their cannonballs then penetrated a larger number of Spanish hulls, complementing damage already done to super-structures. By four o'clock in the afternoon, the Spanish formation was broken, its shattered galleons in no shape to resist demands for sur-render. Massive prize-taking became possible. The English were on the verge of a decisive victory.

But it did not materialize. Suddenly, roaring up from nowhere, a blinding squall so reduced visibility that the threat of collision took first place in every captain's mind. When the downpour ceased, Medina Sidonia was out of English range, once more gallantly reforming his battered but uncaptured force. Too short of shot to risk resuming the battle, the English waited. Heavy weather roiled the sea, and all the while the wind was visibly pressing the Spanish ships towards the sandy Flemish shallows.

TUESDAY, JULY 30: THE BELATED MIRACLE

Overnight the unwilling Armada, pushed by a northwest wind, moved closer and closer to grounding on the Netherlands shore. By morning, the leadsmen taking soundings from its galleons were calling out dangerously diminished numbers as they anxiously heaved their lines. There was no way to stand offshore. Through the fleet, crews were called to make their confessions. The water under the keels was turning brighter and brighter tan. The leadsmen's knots showed seven fath-oms—one fathom equals six feet. Only a little later, they showed six. The next call—full fathom five thy father lies—would be the same as the big ships' draft. In suspense on both sides, everyone waited: which of the Armada's giants would be the first to ground?

There was no grounding. At the ultimate moment, the wind circled considerably more than a third of the compass box, to blow strongly from the south. The weather gauge passed to Medina Sidonia. The Armada's sails filled. He reached for blue water, and found it.

The complete course of the Spanish fleet, up the Channel, through the North Sea, around Scotland and Ireland, and back to Spain.

Philip II had always expected a miracle, and one had been vouchsafed. But this was not the expected miracle, and it came very late. The Enterprise had already failed. Union with Parma was beyond hope now.

For a route home, Medina Sidonia had only a single, sorry possibility. On the wind that saved them, his damaged, thirsty, and hungry fleet could continue to sail—but only northward. Unrepaired and unvictualled ships would have to round the northern islands of Scotland, and cross the top of Ireland, before they could stumble south, under the lash of North Atlantic gales. On the way up the North Sea, northwest winds had threatened them with death on soft sand. On the way down the Irish coast, northwest winds, uncountered by a miracle, would threaten them with death on hard rock, and often carry out the threat; if occasional strong swimmers succeeded in clambering out of the frothing surf they could expect a dubious reception from whoever lived nearby.

Of the galaxy of ships which put to sea from Lisbon in that springtime of 1588, only half came home again, and most of those that finished the course carried sickness and death aboard.

It was some time before the English could be sure that the contest was over. Parma might somehow find an independent way to cross the Channel; Medina Sidonia might somehow find an anchorage where he could repair his damage and return. To quiet this uncertainty, Howard pursued him until he had passed Scotland's Firth of Forth. And as reinsurance against renewal of engagement, when the English turned back, they anchored in ports around the entry to the Thames. It was August 8 before even those who watched and waited at eastern wharfsides could hear a first-hand account of the Armada's passing.

On the same day that the ships came in, Queen Elizabeth, dazzling in red wig and white velvet and mounted on a great dapple-quartered white horse, rode with her train into Tilbury Camp on the north bank of the Thames estuary opposite Gravesend. The outcome of the Enterprise was still uncertain. She came to review troops gathered there against the possibility of an invasion. One of the ballads composed a few weeks later describes her passage downriver:

And on the eight of August she from faire Saint *James'* tooke her way
With many Lords of high degree in princely robes and rich array,
   And to bardge upon the water,
   Being King *Henryes* royall daughter,
She did goe with trumpets sounding, and with dubbing drums apace,
Along the *Thames*, that famous river, for to view the camps a space.

It was a brave show. Yet in encouraging the levies assembled by her
Captain General in scurried haste during recent weeks, the queen must
have fully realized that an encounter between these militia and Parma's
professional troops could hardly be more than a gallant gesture, and in
spite of recent dispatches, it could not be assumed that the Spaniards had
definitively failed. Her purpose was not to celebrate a victory; it was to
reaffirm the unity of English sovereign and English people, the solid and
perennial basis of her reign.

She had been warned that yet another assassination attempt, timed
with the expected arrival of Parma, might that day put her at risk of
physical danger. A current ballad warned possible perpetrators:

> You traitors all that doo devise,
> To hurt our Queene in treacherous wise,
> And in your hartes doo still surmize
>   Which way to hurt our England,
> Consider what the end will be
> Of traitors all in their degree,
> Hanging is still their destenye,
>   That trouble the pease of England.

But the queen repudiated protection; at starting time for the review
she instructed all of her guard, and all but four of the gentlemen who had
accompanied her, to stay where they were. It was a short procession.
Before her, on foot, the earl of Ormonde carried the sword of state. Next
came two young pages: one bore her silver helmet on a pillow; the other
held a lead-strap to her horse. Mounted and flanking her were her
Captain General, Leicester, and her Master of the Horse, Essex. On foot,
behind them, followed the professional soldier Sir John Norreys.

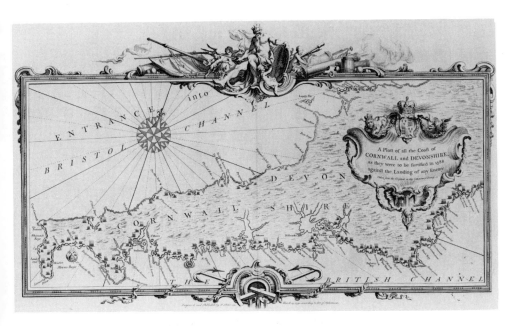

Armed men, recruited by Ralegh and Grenville against invasion, are
shown rimming the English coast.

DETAIL: Bottom center.

The Armada Medal. On the obverse, Elizabeth in bold relief; on the reverse, England's safe and pleasant land.

At walking pace, she passed cheering rank on cheering rank of soldiery. When she spoke it was to voice her care for and her confidence in her people, and her defiance of their common enemy:

My loving people, we have been persuaded by some that are careful for our safety, to take heed how we commit ourselves to armed multitudes, for fear of treachery. But I assure you, I do not desire to live to distrust my faithful and loving people. Let tyrants fear. I have always so behaved myself that, under God, I have placed my chiefest strength and safeguard in the loyal hearts and good will of my subjects; and therefore I am come amongst you as you see, at this time, not for my recreation and disport, but being resolved, in the midst and heat of the battle, to live or die amongst you all, and to lay down for my God and for my kingdom and for my people, my honour and my blood, even in the dust. I know I have the body of a weak and feeble woman, but I have the heart and stomach of a king, and of a king of England too, and think foul scorn that Parma or Spain, or any prince of Europe should dare to invade the borders of my realm; to which, rather than that any dishonour shall grow by me, I myself shall take up arms, I myself will be your general, judge, and rewarder of every one of your virtues in the field.

With evening, as the incoming tide floated bits and pieces of news up the Thames from the suddenly crowded east-coast ports, London could begin a double celebration: the Spanish Armada had ceased to be a threat to English shores; and the Elizabethan compact between sovereign and people had, with royal courage, been resoundingly confirmed.

VII

The Birth of a Navy

 O THE ORDINARY ENGLISHMAN IN HIS PUB, the navy's encounter with the Armada was a great and glorious victory. To him, a ballad that went well with draft ale expressed a simple and obvious fact:

> In eyghtye-eyght, ere I was borne,
>   As I can well remember,
> In August was a fleete prepar'd,
>   The month before September.
>
> Spayne, with Biscayne, Portugall,
>   Toledo and Granado,
> All these did meete, and made a fleete,
>   And call'd it the Armado. . . .
>
> When they had sayl'd along the seas,
>   And anchor'd uppon Dover,
> Our Englishmen did board them then,
>   And cast the Spaniards over.
>
> Our Queen was then at Tilbury,
>   What could you more desire-a?
> For whose sweet sake, Sir Francis Drake
>   Did set them all on fyre-a.
>
> But let them looke about themselves,
>   For if they come again-a,
> They shall be served with that same sauce,
>   As they weere, I know when-a.

Yet after the accounts of the English admirals had been sifted, the running of the Armada appeared in the near view to have been a clouded episode. If wind and water had not intruded at the close of the battle of Gravelines, and if the English ships had not been empty of ammunition when the sudden squall subsided, multiple prize-taking could have scored up a decisive victory. But even the worst-damaged of the Spanish galleons remained uncaptured, and tattered as they were Medina Sidonia led his ships away.

The English themselves had not prevented the junction of Medina Sidonia and Parma; it was faulty preparation that precluded a union of the Spanish forces. Invasion of England had not been repelled; none had been attempted.

Over the long view, however, those ten days in 1588 were perceived to have been decisive. After them, the greatness of Spain as a ranking power was seen to be passing; after them, the greatness of England burgeoned as she became the center of a vast empire.

In retrospect, the real victory of England proved to have been the victory of an idea, a new idea of what men and ships could do. For some years, the concept had been vaguely realized; it shaped itself into a conscious certainty as the ships that Hawkins built responded to the mariners who handled them on the way up the Channel.

To the Spaniards, as in the early years of the century to the English, their galleons were conveyances. Their purpose was to bring fighting men to the scene of battle—of sea battle, after boardings of enemy conveyances, or shore battle after invasion if Spain's enemy were overseas. But now, suddenly, the English saw their ships as weapons. In the past, warships had been operated by mariners who fought at close quarters if their vessels were boarded, but only as auxiliaries of the soldiers who were the military specialists. Now, a true navy was coming into being: the men who handled the ships were the men who framed and carried out the nation's military strategy. In using their ships as weapons, they combined navigational knowledge and skill with military knowledge and skill. A new profession had appeared in English life: that of officer of the Royal Navy.

For the remainder of the war with Spain, for the remainder of Elizabeth's reign, for the remainder of the lifetimes of the great Devonians, English foreign policy was directed by a new concept: control of the seas could destroy the coherence of any empire whose lands were not con-

An Elizabethan warship with the new low profile; above are the Tudor rose
and the initials of Elizabeth Regina.

tiguous. Francis Bacon put it most concisely: "He that commands the
sea is at great Liberty and may take as much or as little of the warre as he
will."

Until the latter 1570s, the English fleets dispatched under the Lord
High Admiral and the Navy Board had patrolled the island's shores and
conveyed troops to places along the Channel and the North Sea, but they
had barely ventured out of sight of land and rarely gone more than a few
days' sail from home ports. Distant use of royal ships, when it occurred,
usually took the form of loans to private explorers and merchants. Royal
awareness was not absent from Drake's circumnavigation, even though
Elizabeth apologized to Philip for this corsair's scandalous behavior, and
the claims to Newfoundland by Gilbert and to Virginia by Grenville
were royally authorized, but the initiative for the voyages came from
their undertakers.

After the Armada, use of the fleet as an instrument of public policy
swiftly increased. From 1589 to the end of the century, voyages to attack
or to blockade the Spanish coast, the Azores, or the cities of the Spanish
Main were almost annual affairs, albeit of varying success. Year after year,
since the discovery of the New World, the shiploads of precious metals
brought home to Philip's royal treasury had financed his diplomacy or his
military operations in Europe. If England's navy destroyed in their home
ports the ships that convoyed this treasure, as Drake had destroyed ships
being readied for the Armada in 1587; if, by blockade, it denied them
use of the Azores for watering and resupply on their way home; if by
either raids on or blockades of Caribbean ports it bottled up the treasure
in harbors there before transport across the ocean could begin, then the
English could nullify main sources of Spanish strength without ever
fighting a land engagement. Recognition of these possibilities became
the foundation of England's post-Armada foreign policy.

For the first months after Gravelines, Drake relished his second helping of national prestige, and this time, in contrast to the months after his
circumnavigation, the court was free to join the rejoicing. He purchased
a long lease on The Herbor, a former royal residence in the Dowgate with

fine gardens leading down to the river. With this acquisition he was possessed of both a town house and a country place suitable for a gentleman, and with these appurtenances he briefly devoted himself to enjoyment of the pleasures of the nouveau riche. His first wife, who died in 1583, had been the seaman Harry Newman's daughter Mary; the present Lady Drake was the heiress of a knight.

Yet by March 1589 he was again on shipboard, heading up a grandiose new enterprise. While in Ireland he had struck up a friendship with the professional soldier Sir John Norreys; together, over the winter, without government participation in its planning and with a private syndicate for its finance, they had projected a flamboyant military-naval operation to restore the kingdom of Portugal to independence and place on its throne Don Antonio, one of the claimants whom Philip had eliminated by his occupation of the country in 1580.

First, they would capture Lisbon, where Don Antonio had assured them that his appearance with English troops would set off an enthusiastic uprising in his favor; and then they would move west to invest the Azores.

As the scheme developed, the queen not only became fully informed, but a major contributor. She advanced £20,000 from her treasury and loaned four of her ships.

Drake's total assemblage of ships of various sizes was greater than that against the Armada, and after sailing he annexed another sixty-five brand-new light-draft Dutch merchantmen that he found in the Channel. Just as he was leaving, the queen ordered him to secure the return of the young Essex, who had stormed away from court in a fit of petulance, but since the favorite was already at sea in Her Majesty's *Swiftsure*, Drake reported he could not lay hands on him—and used the occasion to extract a month's additional royal victualling for his 20,000 men.

Drake's intended destination was Santander. The ships that returned from the Armada were being repaired there, and building for a new Armada had started. But a mistaken impression that Coruña rather than Santander was the center of this effort diverted him to that port as a landing place. When he set Norreys's troops ashore they overcame substantial resistance, captured the galleon *San Juan*, and caused considerable damage, but the operation was accompanied by much indiscipline.

Continuing south, he disembarked the troops again near Peniche, some fifty miles north of Lisbon; thereafter, in approaching the capital, each force would be on its own, unable to communicate with the other. Norreys found the overland going hard, and Drake found the batteries defending Lisbon's harbor formidable. Sickness spread in the fleet. Worst of all, and definitively destructive of the purpose of the expedition, no popular uprising welcomed Don Antonio's attempted return.

Drake's only success was to capture a sixty-ship fleet bringing supplies to Philip from Hanseatic merchants. Back at Peniche, he picked up Norreys and sent him home with the sick as he himself turned towards the Azores where over the years the islanders' attachment to Don Antonio had remained consistently strong. But he did not reach the islands: a gale caused the *Revenge* to spring a serious leak. On July 1, in full anticlimax, he reappeared at Plymouth. Elizabeth was not amused.

It was three years before he received another commission. He spent most of this time in Devon at Buckland; The Herbor was closed. As Plymouth's mayor he improved the town's fortifications, and initiated the piping in of a sorely needed water supply—on April 30 each year, Plymouth still commemorates the day of its opening.

In 1590, Philip blocked any effort to capture the annual *flota* by holding it in the West Indies; in 1591, he assembled so formidable a convoy of the double measure of treasure that the English withdrew from a prospective interception at the Azores; Lord Howard prudently called his ships off from a scene that only Grenville refused to abandon. But in 1592, the strategy of interception justified itself brilliantly in the capture of the *Madre de Dios*.

By 1593, a new Spanish threat to England had materialized: taking advantage of the civil war in France between Protestant Henry of Navarre and the Catholic League supported by Parma's army from the Netherlands, the Spanish had established a base at Brest, on the extreme western end of the Breton peninsula. The location enabled them to exercise surveillance over the Channel, and raised the specter of a new attempt at an English invasion.

The crisis brought Drake back into the queen's favor. He returned to London, reopened The Herbor, and as a member of the 1593 Parliament actively advocated a subsidy of £200,000 for the navy. In the autumn of 1594, Frobisher and Norreys cleared Brest; Frobisher died at Plymouth of ill-tended wounds received in landing Norreys's soldiers.

By 1595, Drake had a naval appointment as co-captain of a new offensive on the Spanish Main. The trouble was that he was a co-captain. The other co-captain was John Hawkins.

Considering the brevity of life-expectancy in the Elizabethan era, Hawkins, now in his mid-sixties, was a very old man. Drake himself was old for those days—around fifty-five—and their styles of fighting, very different even in the days of their youth, had been confirmed by long habit as well as by the lessons of experience as they interpreted them. In co-captaining a voyage the two were certain to clash.

With six royal navy ships—Drake in the *Defiance*, sister ship of the *Revenge*, and Hawkins in the *Garland* of the same class—they set out on August 28, 1595, with twenty-seven sail and 25,000 soldiers commanded by Sir Thomas Baskerville. Hawkins was always a careful victualler; Drake soon found that he was feeding 300 more men than Hawkins from the same amount of rations. Drake wanted to take the Canaries as they passed; Hawkins demurred. But Drake's proposal died at Las Palmas, the main port on Gran Canaria: they found that the Spaniards, apprised of the expedition's departure from England, had barricaded the harbor entrance. After a makeshift stop for water at the western end of the island, Drake and Hawkins started for the West Indies.

Their immediate purpose was to capture a disabled treasure ship said to be in Puerto Rico's San Juan harbor. To relieve it, five Spanish frigates had been sent out; after a storm off Martinique, these captured a small merchantman of the English fleet and tortured the English plans out of its crew. When a second English ship, witness to the capture, brought the news to a rendezvous, Drake was for racing the Spaniards to San

Juan; Hawkins insisted that they should first ready their ships for battle after their transatlantic crossing, and his counsel found support among the other captains. It was ten days before they approached San Juan. During the approach, Hawkins sickened and died.

Drake, now in sole command, attempted a middle-aged revival of his youth. His bravado was unimpaired, but the split-second timing that had terrorized the Spanish cities no longer complemented it. When, with the old impudence, he anchored within reach of the Spanish guns at San Juan harbor, the stool on which he sat was shot out from under him, and the two officers beside him were killed. When the Spanish sank a ship to block the harbor, he observed a narrow way still open around its end, but they completed the barrier before he moved. The treasure remained intact.

The next—and major—purpose of the voyage was to revive his plan of 1585–86 and cut the Spanish possessions in two at the Isthmus. He dawdled, turning to ravage Rio de la Hacha and other eastern Caribbean towns while word of his presence accelerated preparations for fending him off in the west. The damage he had done a decade earlier had convinced Philip of the need to divert some of his treasure from shipments home to strengthen local fortifications in the west. Drake disembarked Baskerville's soldiers at Nombre de Dios, but the force was not strong enough to take Panama.

On pulling out, he stopped at a small island to water and careen. The place was pestilence-ridden, and Drake's body was no longer able to resist the tropical infections to which it had formerly been immune. He succumbed to, and could not throw off, a fever.

On January 27, 1596, he called for his unsigned will and summoned his wife's nephew, Captain Jonas Bodenham, and his own brother Thomas, soon to be the last survivor of Edmund Drake's twelve sons, to witness his completion of it. That night, delirious, he struggled to his feet and demanded to be dressed in his armor; he knew he was going to die, and he wanted to die in harness. Later he lay down again, finally.

For his funeral, two ships for which the depleted expedition no longer had sufficient crews floated as ceremonial fireships on the quiet sea. The

Drake's drum, bought new for his circumnavigation,
was painted with his coat of arms after he
was knighted.

drum, still preserved at Buckland Abbey, that Drake had bought new for his round-the-world voyage, and painted with the arms that Elizabeth granted him on its completion, beat a funereal measure. Trumpets sounded a last salute as the leaden coffin tilted and slipped into the waters that as corsair and commander Drake had traversed for a quarter-century.

Failure and death thus closed the careers of two of the great captains who had been most effective advocates of the new concept of naval power. But within six months of their passing, in an expedition under Howard and Essex, Sir Walter Ralegh, essentially repeating Drake's pre-Armada raid on Cadiz of 1587, carried through the most telling demonstration of what a fleet operated according to their new strategy could accomplish.

It was Ralegh, too, who wrote the clearest definition of what the captains of Elizabeth's reign had come to understand: "Whosoever commands the sea commands the trade; whosoever commands the trade of the world commands the riches of the world, and consequently the world itself."

VIII

The Renaissance Man

IR WALTER RALEGH WAS DIFFERENT FROM THE others. He was a captain, but he was also a courtier. He was a Devon man, but he was also a London personality. He was deeply learned in the sciences on which navigators relied to guide them on transoceanic voyages, but he was as well a poet whose lyrics time has not surprised. His life was one of the prisms that spread into rainbow colors the intense white light of the Renaissance.

His boyhood belonged wholly to Devon and the sea. Ralegh's birthplace, leased by his father for many years and little changed today, was the large, comfortable farmhouse of Hayes Barton, near the south Devon coast, a mile west of the village of East Budleigh. In his youth, East Budleigh was a little port on the River Otter, twinned by Otterton across the estuary. But while most of the time Devon enjoys many of the soft, misty mornings that keep England a green and pleasant land, occasional sudden thunderstorms, like Channel squalls, pour flash floods down the red clay of Devon's rolling hillsides, silting up its river beds. As a result, East Budleigh and Otterton today look at each other across fertile fields watered by a narrow stream; but as lads in the sixteenth century, the Ralegh boys could clamber in and out of boats on the more substantial river near their home and gain a feel for seamanship.

Starting in his teens, however, Walter Ralegh lived his life at a different level from most of the other great Devonians. He and his half brother Humphrey Gilbert were the only university men among them; at Oriel College, Oxford, Walter studied among dons and fellow students absorbed in the new sciences—mathematics, astronomy, geography, cosmology—that in turn were applicable to the art of ocean navigation. Thomas Harriot, his lifelong friend and associate, was one of these, and Richard Hakluyt, a divinity student at Christ Church College, was the man who collected the accounts of the sixteenth-century voyages that are a main source of their history.

After attending Oxford, many young men, Ralegh among them, enrolled at London's Inns of Court. The Inns served as intellectual clubs—some of their members had no serious intention of becoming barristers. With such companions, the young Devonian—he never lost his West Country accent—enjoyed the life of young-men-about-town; they fought a forbidden duel or two, tangled with the law occasionally because of their or their servants' misbehavior, preened themselves in extravagant dress, wrote some verse. When George Gascoigne obtained the patronage of the earl of Leicester for his new publication, *The Steel Glass*, Ralegh wrote a prefatory sonnet.

Humphrey Gilbert introduced his half brother at court, and brought him to the notice of Sir Francis Walsingham. In the early '70s, Ralegh soldiered for four years in France, along with his mother's cousin, Gawain Champernoune, under the Protestant Comte de Montgomerie. At the start of Gilbert's first voyage, he captained the queen's *Falcon*; when the rest of the fleet was driven back by storms, he stayed out and captured some Spaniards—but with damage to Her Majesty's ship that required explanation on his return. At the end of the decade, he was a company commander in Ireland under Lord Grey of Wilton. When Italian and Spanish soldiers, under the pope's flag, arrived at Smerwick to aid the Irish, he was one of two duty officers in charge of an ensuing slaughter, in which some six hundred Catholic troops were cut down.

Up to this point, Ralegh's life had been similar to that of many young gentlemen of his time, but in the late autumn of 1581, when a number of English companies, including his, were disbanded, he returned to England bearing dispatches to the queen—and like a brilliant comet entering a region of fixed stars, he suddenly illumined the court. At the opening of the great decade of a great reign, the rapidity of the rise of this commoner from Devon startled his sovereign's aristocratic entourage and incited envy in broader circles.

Her Majesty was ready for a new favorite. Two years before, the Spanish ambassador, with delicate malice, had revealed Lord Leicester's

Sir Walter Ralegh.

secret marriage to Lettice Knollys, the widow of the first earl of Essex. Red-haired like herself, this granddaughter of Anne Boleyn's sister Mary was Elizabeth's far-from-favorite cousin. Leicester, long as central a figure at the court as Burghley and Walsingham were on the Privy Council, was a scion of one of the kingdom's most powerful families. He was Robert Dudley, the fifth of six sons of John Dudley, duke of Northumberland, who at the accession of Elizabeth's half sister had attempted to merge the royal line with his own by marrying his fourth son, Guilford, to a rival claimant to Queen Mary's throne, the Lady Jane Grey—and brought himself and the young couple to the scaffold.

For years, Robert had been Elizabeth's support, solace, and courtly lover. After Leicester's marriage was dissolved by the mysterious death of his wife Amy Robsart—she was found with her neck broken at the foot of the imposing stairs at Cumnor Place—there had even been talk that the court might shortly witness a new alliance. It did, but the woman in the case was the queen's cousin, not the queen.

Elizabeth's life had had in it very little of love: at her father's direction, her mother had been dispatched at the executioner's block before she was three, and two subsequent stepmothers had respectively been divorced and beheaded before she was ten. In her early teens, Lord Thomas Seymour, the brother of the Lord Protector Somerset who had taken charge of the government during the minority of Edward VI, had molested her when she was a member of his household. And, toward the end of Mary's reign, the political intrigues of her retainer, Katherine Champernoune, and her husband in regard to the succession had caused Elizabeth to undergo perilous interrogation before being cleared of suspicion of treason.

Ralegh's arrival was thus superbly, if inadvertently, timed. After a few years, the queen again welcomed Leicester by her side, but he was by that time a middle-aged companion. At the opening of the '80s, Elizabeth, then forty-eight years old, was walking through empty rooms, and Ralegh, in the prime of youth, appeared and filled them.

He was indeed personable. The words of the gossipy John Aubrey, "Q. Elizabeth loved to have all the servants of her court proper men, and (as

Robert Dudley, earl of Leicester.

before said) Sr. W. R.s gracefule presence was no mean recommendation to him," were corroborated by the brush of Nicholas Hilliard, the Devon artist who introduced the miniature to English Renaissance painting: the darkly haunting, sensitive face appears above a finely pointed beard encircled by a lace-edged ruff. Other portraits show his entire figure set off in the latest fashion down to his pearl-embroidered slippers—fit attire to adorn the court of a queen whose attendants consorted with her title of Gloriana. (In 1584, when Ralegh became a member of Parliament, his jesting colleagues appointed him to a committee considering means of reducing current extravagance in dress.)

Later in the century a German traveler, Paul Hentzner, on a visit to Elizabeth's court, set down a meticulous description of the scene in which Ralegh quickly came to move with assurance. The queen, at her favorite palace of Greenwich, attended Sunday service, and then returned to dinner:

First went Gentlemen, Barons, Earls, Knights of the Garter, all richly dressed and bare-headed; next came the Chancellor, bearing the Seals in a red-silk Purse, between Two; one of which carried the Royal Sceptre, the other the Sword of State, in a red scabbard, flushed with golden Fleurs de Lis, the point upwards: next came the Queen in the Sixty-fifth year of her Age, as we are told, very majestic; her Face oblong, fair, but wrinkled; her Eyes small, yet black and pleasant; her Nose a little hooked; her Lips narrow, and her Teeth black (a defect the English seem subject to, from their too great use of sugar); she had in her Ears two pearls with very rich drops; she wore false hair, and that red; upon her Head she had a small Crown, reported to be made of the gold of the celebrated Lunebourg table. Her Bosom was uncovered, as all the English ladies have it, till they marry; and she had on a Necklace of exceeding fine jewels; her Hands were small, her Fingers long, and her Stature neither tall nor low; her air was stately, her manner of speaking mild and obliging. That day she was dressed in white Silk, bordered with pearls of the size of beans, and over it a Mantle of black silk shot with silver threads; her Train was very long, the end of it borne by a Marchioness; instead of a Chain, she had an oblong Collar of gold and jewels. As she went along in all her state and magnificence, she spoke very graciously, first to one, then to another, whether foreign Ministers, or those who attended for different reasons, in English, French and Italian, being well skilled in Greek, Latin, and the languages I have mentioned, she is mistress of Spanish, Scotch and Dutch: Whoever speaks to her, it is kneeling; now and then she raises some with her Hand . . .

. . . While she was still at Prayers, we saw her Table set out with the following Solemnity:

A Gentleman entered the room bearing a rod, and along with him another who had a table-cloth, which after they had both kneeled three times, with the utmost veneration, he spread upon the table, and after kneeling again, they both retired. Then came two others, one with the rod again, the other with a salt-cellar, a plate and bread; when they had kneeled, as the others had done, and placed what was brought upon the table, they two retired with the same ceremonies performed by the first. At last came an unmarried Lady (we were told she was a Countess) and along with a married one, bearing a tasting-knife, who when she had prostrated herself three times, in the most graceful manner approached the table, and rubbed the plates with bread and salt, with as much awe as if the Queen had been present: When they had waited there a little while, the Yeomen of the Guard entered, bareheaded, clothed in scarlet with a golden rose upon their backs, bringing in at each turn a course of 24 dishes, served in plate, most of it gilt; these dishes were received by a gentleman in the same order they were brought and placed upon the table, while the Lady-taster gave to each of the guard a mouthful to eat for fear of any poison. During the time that this guard, which consists of the tallest and stoutest men that can be found in all England, being carefully selected for this service, were bringing dinner, twelve trumpets and two kettle drums made the hall ring for half an hour together.

Ralegh's skill with his quill gave him a special advantage as he joined the press of courtiers flattering the queen's vanity. His words struck just the right balance between forwardness and deference:

> Our Passions are most like to Floods and streames:
> The shallow Murmure, but the Deep are Dumb;
> So when Affections yeeld Discourse, it seems
> The bottom is but shallow whence they come.
> They that are Rich in Words, in words discover
> That they are Poore in that which makes a lover.
>
> Wrong not, deare Empresse of my Heart,
> The Meritt of true Passion,
> With thinking that Hee feels no Smart,
> That sues for no Compassion . . .

Silence in Love bewraies more Woe
   Than Words, though ne'er so Witty;
A Beggar that is dumb, yee know,
   Deserveth double Pitty.
Then misconceive not, (dearest Heart)
   My true, though secret Passion;
Hee smarteth most that hides his smart,
   And sues for no Compassion.

The queen was entranced. Over the next years, Ralegh sparkled in a continuous shower of her gifts. For a London residence, she granted him spacious apartments (all but the street floor, occupied by a cousin) in Durham House, where she herself had lived for a time as a princess, and where Lady Jane Grey enacted her tragedy as royal claimant. One of its high turrets served Ralegh as a study overlooking the Thames; the grounds extended from the Strand to the riverside. There was stabling for forty horses. Until Henry VIII's time, this had been the London palace of the Durham bishops.

As income to maintain this state, Elizabeth endowed her new companion with the lucrative monopolies of licensing wine retailers and broadcloth exporters. Next came a knighthood. Western honors followed: Warden of the Stannaries, whose courts at the Devon towns of Tavistock, Chagford, Ashburton, and Plympton heard disputes and governed the weighing and stamping of West Country tin; Lord Lieutenant (the sovereign's representative) in Cornwall; Vice Admiral of Cornwall and Devon.

When English colonization was attempted in Ireland, letters patent conveyed to Ralegh very large acreages in the counties of Cork and Waterford, with 40,000 reserved for his private use; in 1587, her gift of the confiscated estates of Anthony Babington, a plotter against her life, made him a substantial English landowner. Small wonder that eyebrows were raised by members of noble families accustomed over generations to share among themselves the perquisites their sovereign could distribute. Ralegh's family was, and for generations had been, of good Devon stock, but they were untitled gentry: at court he was a social

On the left is Durham House on the Thames, granted by Elizabeth for
Ralegh's residence in the early 1580s.

interloper. Viewing developments, the court jester, Richard Tarleton,
coined a phrase enjoyed by card-playing discontents: "See, the knave
commands the queen."

But at this stage in his life, Ralegh, who was not always judicious in
choosing his friends, did not have to be so: he was part of the inner circle
for whom the queen devised pet names. Leicester had always been her
"Eyes"; Sir Christopher Hatton, her Captain of the Guard, her "Mut-
ton"; for Ralegh's nickname, she dropped the "l" to approximate the
West Country pronunciation and make him her "Water"—that was why
he projected an epic to be titled "The Book of the Ocean to Cynthia."

In her serious moods, his intellectual interests commended him
equally to the learned queen; at Durham House he assembled men from
many fields of the New Learning. At this and later periods of his life,
Henry Percy, the earl of Northumberland, known as "the wizard earl"

because of his scientific interests, was close to Ralegh; so was John Dee, who had lectured in Paris on Euclid and traveled the Continent for consultations with such savants as Gerard Mercator, from whom Dee obtained a brand-new map of the world and at Elizabeth's request prepared for her descriptions of the new geography revealed by recent discoveries. Ralegh engaged Thomas Harriot to join his personal entourage as his mathematics tutor, and sent him to America to spend a year in scientific observation with his first colonists. When French Huguenot refugees settled in London after the Spanish drove them out of Florida, he subsidized the artist Jacques le Moyne de Mourges who had been in the New World with them on a similar errand. The watercolorist John White illustrated his attempted settlements at Roanoke. (The work of these three men comprises the first description of North America as it was when the Europeans came.)

Ralegh's library was like others in which the sudden expansion of physical knowledge was visibly evidenced not only by books but by a variety of unfamiliar apparatus—astrolabes, globes, retorts, the test fires of assayists. These, and the parallel enthusiasm for astrology, alchemy, and the occult of John Dee and many other scientists, invited unrest among the superstitious and the ignorant. Christopher Marlowe's *Doctor Faustus* gave expression in the theater to a mood in the agora that was ominous and dangerous for those who took part in uninhibited speculation; clashes between the new knowledge and the old verities gave Ralegh's sessions the name of "The School of Night"; and later accusations of atheism against him, extending to a charge of harboring a coven of warlocks, found their sources in these scientific sessions. A widely translated Latin attack on him by a Jesuit priest, Father Robert Parsons, strengthened such charges; a libel of uncertain authorship assures its reader that

> *Raw* is the reason that doth *lie*
> Within an atheist's head,
> Which saith the soul of man doth die,
> When that the body's dead.

MEVM PECCATVM SI BONVM.
DEI DONVM
SI MALVM
Anno

Francisco Delaram sculp.

Of Art and Nature, see the mytuall Ties:
As Nature into Art her Life exhales;
So Art in Nature, her defects supplies,
And thus to each, are Both Reciprocalls.
No Face moues so, with all Proportions parts
As Manners well compos'd, & numerous harts
Geo: Chapman

Thomas Harriot.

During the queen's great decade, Elizabeth stifled Ralegh's aspirations as a navigator by keeping him by her side: she stayed him from sailing with Humphrey Gilbert in 1583; she stayed him from leading his colonists to America in 1585 and 1587; he did not receive a naval command either for the Armada in 1588, or in 1591, when he had hoped to be vice admiral under Lord Howard on his voyage to the Azores. His cousin Richard Grenville was his replacement on the *Tiger* in 1585, and in 1591 on the *Revenge*. His first printed publication, a *Report of the Truth of the Fight about the Iles of Acores this last Summer*, immortalized Grenville's death on the second mission.

Yet Elizabeth's generosity to her courtier never extended to a position of substantive policy-making. When she promoted her cousin Lord Hunsdon from the post of Captain of the Guard to that of Lord Chamberlain in 1583, she put Ralegh in charge of the yeomen responsible for her personal safety. Required, then, to be in the queen's proximity, he walked resplendent as the court's famous faces were reflected in his silver armor. But the Privy Council was where Ralegh would have liked to have been, to help clarify national public purposes along with Burghley and Walsingham, and a place there was never offered him. The queen thought of him as a poet and a courtier—perhaps even as a bit of a dilettante—a man more capable of brilliant intuition than a man of sober judgment like Lord Burghley.

So his influence remained potent but private: in 1583 he persuaded Her Majesty not to carry through a sudden impulse to cancel Humphrey Gilbert's voyage; after the Armada, when all English shipping was confined to home ports, he obtained her permission for a relief fleet to sail to his Roanoke colony.

In maritime circles, he effectively advocated the changes in ship design to which Hawkins gave effect in time for the Armada. Years later, he summarized those changes in a report for the Stuart heir apparent, Henry, Prince of Wales: a warship 100 feet long and thirty-five feet wide was the best size. High-charged ships were outdated: two decks and a half above the orlop were enough—at sea "a man may not expect the ease of many cabins." Ships that are sheathed do not have to be caulked and

Queen Elizabeth standing on a map of England, with the southern
counties, including Devon, before her.

Ralegh in silver armor as Elizabeth's Captain of the Guard.

repaired every year. The recent placement of the galley in the forecastle instead of at the bottom of the ship on merchantmen reduces the danger of fire and the noisomeness of the hold, and should be imitated on warships.

During periods when he was barred from court, Ralegh kept his ideas before the public eye as an M.P. He was elected to four of Elizabeth's last six Parliaments; in that of 1593 few speakers other than the Lord Chancellor addressed the House of Commons more often than he. He proved a skillful debater on substantive matters, as when he supported Elizabeth's requests for subsidies for defense but opposed regressive taxation in providing them. He was likewise adept at meeting private attack: as the popular grumbling over Elizabeth's dispensation of monopolies grew, he blunted censure of his own generous supply by citing his successful conduct as Warden of the Stannaries: in that office, he had worked out a means of stabilizing metal prices that conferred substantial benefits alike on miners and on the entire industry.

When the decade of the '90s brought change that was poignant to Ralegh, the time was no less wrenching to the queen. All around her, English foreign relations were not going well. Philip's failure of 1588 was not yet seen as definitive. Though only half of the Armada's ships returned to Spain, some sixty-five of them managed to do so, a by-no-means inconsiderable fleet, and he was ordering extensive new building. The greatest among Spain's post-Armada ships were the twelve named for the Apostles; the 1,500-ton *St. Philip* had been the first to attack Grenville's *Revenge*. The English sacked Cadiz in 1596, but the Spaniards occupied Calais. Two more Armadas were loosed against England, and the last, in 1599, got as close as The Lizard before storms drove it away. When the Irish rose in Tyrone's rebellion, Spain sent help. Peace with Spain was not signed in Elizabeth's lifetime.

In France, after the assassination of Henry III in 1589, open war between his then-Protestant successor, Henry of Navarre, and the Guises' Catholic League required active English help. The cost of sending an initial 4,000 troops, doubled later and then reinforced again, continually drained the treasury. When Parma's army came down from the Netherlands to aid the League, another 4,000 English had to be sent to Rouen. Spanish troops appeared in Brittany and stayed there. Only after Henry IV had found Paris worth a mass did this drain subside.

In all the surrounding lands, Elizabeth's only confirmed success was that of the 6,000 troops she had kept in the deep-water ports of the Netherlands at a cost of some £126,000 a year; by 1595 the forces of Maurice of Nassau had consolidated control firmly enough for the northern provinces to assume independence as a country with borders corresponding to those of Holland today. Yet the political success had an economic counterweight: Dutch competition for overseas trade reduced the profits of English merchants.

Debt, Elizabeth's perennial horror, increased from year to year. When she died in 1603, an estimate of the Crown's expenditures on wars since 1585 set the total at some £4 million; to meet this, Parliamentary subsidies averaged little more than £112,000 in their peak years of 1599–1601. The queen and Burghley had cleared her inherited debt, and accumulated savings of £300,000 during the decade before 1585, but war costs had wiped them out, and after some £800,000 of Crown lands (as well as numerous monopolies) had been sold, levies of troops and equipment required of the localities, feudal dues and other perquisites scrupulously exacted, a £400,000 debt was still outstanding.

In the late 1580s and during the 1590s, moreover, practically all of Elizabeth's trusty and well-beloved longtime advisers, from great sea-captains to court favorites to Privy Councillors, preceded her in death. Leicester died in 1588, not long after they rode together at Tilbury; her Chancellor of the Exchequer, Sir Walter Mildmay, in 1589; her intelligence officer, Sir Francis Walsingham, in 1590; her Lord Chancellor and favorite, Sir Christopher Hatton, in 1591; Henry Carey, Lord Hunsdon, her first cousin and her Lord Chamberlain, in 1596. Of her sea-captains, Grenville died in 1591, Frobisher in 1594, Hawkins and Drake in 1595–96. Her main reliance of forty years, Lord Burghley, departed this world and her service in 1598. And in 1601, an execution that she herself ordered ended the life of her final favorite on a charge of treason.

Essex, the new court sensation.

This last of the men for whom she deeply cared was Robert Devereux, second earl of Essex. Through his maternal grandmother, Mary Boleyn, young Essex was closely related to the queen, but—ironically enough— it was his tie to Leicester, his stepfather, that brought him into the intimate court circle. The youth's blond handsomeness was a foil to Ralegh's dark beauty; he had the appealing eye and the sulky lips of a spoiled child. In 1589, he was about twenty-three and Ralegh about thirty-seven, as Ralegh had been about twenty-nine and Leicester about forty-nine in 1581. Her Majesty became openly infatuated, and her Captain of the Guard had to stand by and watch the attachment to his new rival grow.

Characteristically, Elizabeth vacillated from one to the other. Ralegh might be delighted to overhear her sharply rebuking his rival for spoken derogation of him and watch while a childishly furious Essex rushed out of her sight, shouting over his shoulder that he would "go and die in the wars in Holland," only to be brought back like a chastised puppy. Yet Essex's strength was so obviously on the rise that in 1589 Ralegh retired to his Irish estates. There, he reconstructed his castle at Lismore and visited his fellow poet Edmund Spenser at Kilcolman. It was perhaps at this time that he distilled his bitterness in a poem unlike his other works that begins:

> Goe soule the bodies guest
>   upon a thankelesse arrant,
> Feare not to touch the best,
>   the truth shall be thy warrant.
> Goe since I needs must die,
>   and give the world the lie.
>
> Say to the Court it glowes
>   and shines like rotten wood,
> Say to the Church it showes
>   what's good, and doth no good:
> If Church and Court reply,
>   then give them both the lie . . .

Yet rotten or not, the court was a continuing magnet. While he was at

Kilcolman, he and Spenser composed prefatory sonnets for Spenser's *Faerie Queen*, and in 1590 the two returned to London for presentation of Spenser's work to Elizabeth. (She horrified Burghley by the extravagance of her gracious award to the author: "Fifty pounds for a poem?" he snorted.)

They came at a fortunate moment: Ralegh's rival had just suffered a setback. Following his stepfather's example, Essex had contracted a secret marriage, with Walsingham's daughter and Philip Sidney's widow, Frances. Inevitably, Elizabeth found out. Since marriages within her intimate circle, especially secret ones, unfailingly exasperated the Virgin Queen, she forbade Essex the court, and turned to Ralegh. In 1591, she named him her vice admiral for an ambush of the Spanish fleet. But when the time came, she did not let him go; it was Grenville who sailed in his place for the confrontation in which the only English ship that fought was the *Revenge*.

The following winter, however, Ralegh's chance appeared to be at hand when a joint-stock venture was set up to attempt once again to carry out the plan that had failed the previous year. The queen would supply two ships and £3,000; George Clifford, earl of Cumberland, six ships; London merchants, two; Carew and Walter Ralegh, one each. Ralegh spent the next months at Chatham, investing almost all of his own capital, and borrowing more; twelve ships, including his *Roebuck*, were poised at the ready when the sailing date was delayed by a contrary wind. During the delay, Elizabeth decided to substitute Frobisher for Ralegh. But stiff-necked Frobisher, though an excellent navigator, was an unpopular commander; murmurs of dissatisfaction caused the queen to allow Ralegh to accompany the fleet as far as Finisterre on the northwest coast of Spain. They sailed in May 1592, but Ralegh immediately received a sharp recall. He sent a squadron to watch the Azores, and came home.

Again, a secret marriage by a favorite had infuriated the queen; this time, Ralegh was the bridegroom. Eight years earlier, Bess Throckmorton, daughter of Elizabeth's ambassador to Paris and sister of Elizabeth's faithful courtier Sir Arthur Throckmorton, had been appointed one of

Her Majesty's maids of honor. As Captain of the Guard, Ralegh constantly saw the maids, and the captain had fallen in love.

In one of his passages on Ralegh, John Aubrey depicts him engaged in passing dalliance:

> He loved a wench well, and one time getting up one of the maids-of-honour up against a tree in the wood ('twas his first lady), who seemed at first boarding to be something fearful of her honour and modest, she cried, "Sweet Sir Walter, what do you me ask? Will you undo me? Nay, sweet Sir Walter! Sweet Sir Walter! Sir Walter!" At last, as the danger and the pleasure at the same time grew higher, she cried in the ecstasy, "Swisser Swatter, Swisser Swatter!" She proved with child.

That was not the only occasion when an amatory impulse on Ralegh's part had a consequence. Among bequests listed in a will drafted in 1597 and found in recent years in the Sherborne archives, Ralegh specified a sum of 500 marks for "My Reputed Daughter begotten on the body of Alice Goold now in Ireland." The diary of one Elie Brevint of the island of Sark further indicates that when Ralegh was governor of Jersey he found the girl a titled husband in the person of a young man in his care, Daniel Dumarez, Seigneur de Saumarez.

But his relation to Bess Throckmorton, though she became pregnant before their marriage, differed as much from previous casual contacts as it did from his platonic attachment to the queen.

The poetry that he wrote Bess is not like his former lyrics, addressed to his chaste Diana, his immortal Cynthia, moon-goddess above touch by mortal men:

> Praisd be Dianas faire and harmles light,
> Praisd be the dewes wherwith she moists the ground;
> Praisd be hir beames, the glorie of the night,
> Praisd be hir powre, by which all powres abound.

By contrast, the woman that Ralegh celebrated in the 1590s was of flesh and blood, held and beheld in passionate intimacy:

> Nature that washt her hands in milke
> And had forgot to dry them,
> In stead of earth tooke snow and silke,

Bess Throckmorton, Queen Elizabeth's maid-of-honor who became
Sir Walter Ralegh's wife.

At Loves request to trye them,
If she a mistresse could compose
To please Loves fancy out of those.

Her eyes he would should be of light,
    A Violett breath, and Lips of Jelly,
Her haire not blacke, nor over bright,
    And of the softest downe her Belly;
As for her inside hee'ld have it
Only of wantonnesse and witt . . .

Yet she was held and beheld also in the somber urgency of a lover haunted
by the silent slipping of sand through the hourglass:

O cruell Time which takes in trust
    Our youth, our Joyes and all we have,
And payes us but with age and dust:
    Who in the darke and silent grave
When we have wandred all our wayes
Shutts up the story of our dayes.

Neither of the Raleghs behaved well after the news became known.
Bess had become pregnant in 1591; the date of their marriage is not of
record. In 1592, at the time of her child's expected birth, Walter was in
Falmouth, where the fleet that he had organized over the winter was just
about to sail. He had written Sir Robert Cecil a barefaced lie denying
current rumors: "I mean not to come away, as they say I will, for fear of a
marriage and I know not what. If any such thing were, I would have
imparted it unto yourself before any man living; and therefore I pray
believe it not, and I beseech you to suppress what you can any such
malicious report. For I protest before God, there is no one on the face of
the earth that I would be fastened onto."

And Bess, as soon as the child could be put out to nurse, slipped back
into her place among the maids as though nothing had happened.

But the queen knew, and to her, while the seduction might be
dismissed as regrettable, the secret marriage was unforgivable.

Perhaps the most bizarre of all the events surrounding little Demarei

The Tower of London, where Ralegh was confined briefly by Elizabeth and for nearly thirteen years by James I.

Ralegh's birth was the appearance, at his christening on April 10, 1592, of Essex to join the Throckmortons as the child's godfather.

At the end of May, Ralegh was back in London, and his son was brought to Durham House to be shown to his father. (The baby must have died very young—no further mention is made of him.)

The queen herself remained ominously silent, but before the month was out, Ralegh was under house arrest, and in August, when Her Majesty left London on her summer progress, both Raleghs were sent to the Tower, where her former companion on those pleasant summer visitations wrote that his "heart never broke till this day."

The previous January, during the Christmas revels, Elizabeth had bestowed on the man who was now her prisoner a ninety-nine-year lease on Sherborne Abbey in Dorset for his country residence; at the end of June, even though all was known, he nevertheless received confirmation of the gift. He had long wanted a home in the west. Seven or eight years earlier, he had attempted to buy his birthplace at Hayes Barton from one Richard Duke whose family owned it as part of a large estate acquired through a purchase of monastic lands. But they had refused his offer. Thereafter, as he journeyed back and forth over the road between London and the West Country, his eyes had fallen on Sherborne.

Historically, the Abbey was the property of the bishopric of Old Sarum, but the queen, after negotiations with an about-to-be-appointed bishop, had succeeded in obtaining it. On the news of its transfer, local people recalled an evil omen: when St. Osmund founded the abbey four hundred years earlier, he had laid a curse on whosoever should violate this holy ground, and the companions riding with Ralegh when he first looked at it recalled that his horse, slipping on the clayey, rain-soaked road, had reared and tossed him flat on his face in the mud at the entrance. Now Ralegh had the property, but not the liberty to enjoy it.

Yet only a bare month after Elizabeth had put Ralegh in the Tower, events constrained her to order him out again. The squadron that he had sent to watch for prizes at the Azores had found one: the Portuguese freighter *Madre de Dios*, homing from the Orient. Seven decks deep, every deck crammed with precious cargo, she was the greatest prize the English ever took. Hawkins, whose *Dainty* was one of the captors, estimated that when taken, her value was not less than £500,000.

But that was not her value when she was brought into port at Dartmouth: the crews who boarded her at the Azores had meanwhile helped themselves, and many of their ships had scurried to other anchorages where they could unload their loot without benefit of the exciseman.

The Privy Council had sent Burghley's son, Sir Robert Cecil, west to keep watch over proceedings, but his diminutive figure did not impress, much less quell, the robust and busy spoilers. As Navy Treasurer,

Hawkins advised the Council that the only way to secure the queen's share was to send Ralegh to Dartmouth with all speed. It was a difficult decision: Elizabeth was an injured woman, but she was also an avaricious Tudor. She sent Ralegh.

Cecil was volubly surprised at the effect of the Devonian's arrival. With what Ralegh saved from the looters and what he forced them to disgorge, ship and contents still brought £141,200. But the queen's continued displeasure with him was clearly evidenced by the division of the spoils. She herself took £80,000; the London investors doubled their money; the Ralegh brothers, who had put in £34,000, part of which was borrowed at interest, were allowed only £36,000.

But though he had traveled under guard, Ralegh was out of the Tower, and by year's end, Bess too had been released. In happy anticipation, they departed for Sherborne. One of the poems attributed to Ralegh reads:

> Now, Serena, be not coy,
> Since we freely may enjoy
> Sweet embraces, such delights
> As will shorten tedious nights. . . .
> Nature her bounties will bestow
> On us that we might use them. And
> 'Tis coldness not to understand
> What she and youth and form persuade
> With opportunity that's made
> As we could wish it. . . .

Over the next few years, the couple lavished money on abbey and grounds, and built a splendid new house. The abbey walls, and the lovely interlaced interior Norman arches and decorated columns, were then in good condition—the damage visible today was the work of Cromwell's guns in the next century—but after a time, the Raleghs decided that the building was damp. In the field beyond the abbey's moat they put up the central tower of the great house that is Sherborne now. Their elaborate landscaping included diversion of water from the River Yeo; Adrian Gilbert lent his good offices in designing it. In 1593, a new son, Wat Ralegh, was born there. The home in the west that his father had long wanted was a reality.

Yet Ralegh could not be satisfied with purely domestic interests. In post-Armada policy-making at the Privy Council, a new venture against Spain with which he was deeply concerned began to receive attention. After Philip took over Portugal and its assets, he had not actively exploited the area called Guiana in the Orinoco River watershed. By occupying it, England might drive a wedge between New Spain and the former Portuguese settlements in eastern Brazil. Rumors circulated of a kingdom comparable in richness to that of the Incas; its name was Manoa, and El Dorado, its king, was believed to bathe in turpentine and then be dusted with gold. Ralegh longed to seek the place—and the gold mine—and plant Elizabeth's standard there; the prospect became an obsession with him.

In 1594 he sent his captain, Jacob Whiddon, on a reconnaissance trip to scout the Spanish-held island of Trinidad, opposite the Orinoco's delta. The next year, Ralegh wrote *The Discourse of the Large, Rich and Beautiful Empire of Guiana*, dedicated jointly to Lord Howard and to Burghley's unmistakably rising son, Sir Robert Cecil. Harriot drew a map to accompany it. Public imagination was inflamed: the book went through three reprintings in the year 1596, and one Dutch, two Latin, and four German editions came out over the next five years. Some strange phenomena were attributed to the area—Chapman's ode *De Guiana* mentions among them "The Anthropophagi; the men whose heads / Do grow beneath their shoulders." But the main attraction was the gold mine.

Having received letters patent for a voyage, in February 1595, with 150 men in five ships plus a converted Spanish galleon, Ralegh crossed the Atlantic himself for the first time. His company included several relatives: Humphrey Gilbert's son John, Grenville's son John, their cousin Butshead Gorges. The naval commander Amyas Preston, and George Somers, discoverer of the Bermudas, asked to go; Leicester's illegitimate son, Sir Robert Dudley, planned to join them at Trinidad.

Ralegh and his son Wat, 1602.

Ralegh's scientific adviser, Lawrence Keymiss of Balliol College, Oxford, was the Harriot of the expedition.

At Trinidad they captured Don Antonio de Berreo, the Spanish governor who had killed some of Whiddon's men the year before, burned the town, and set off up the Orinoco with an old Indian chief as guide. Though they traveled many jungle miles, they did not find Manoa; by September they were home with only some worthless ore samples believed to be the matrix of gold deposits. But they were not in the least discouraged.

The war with Spain continued. Two months after his return, Ralegh urged the Privy Council to permit him to gather a fleet to inspect the Spanish coast for what Philip might be preparing. Essex became attached to the project. On June 3, 1596, commanded by Howard and Essex, ninety-six English and twenty-two Dutch ships, with 10,000 soldiers brought back from France under Sir Francis Vere, set out for Cadiz. The fleet was divided into four squadrons, equipped, for the first time on record, with their own distinguishing flags—white, orange tawny, blue, and crimson, forerunners of the red, white, and blue ensigns of the main, fore, and rear squadrons shortly established by the English navy. Essex was in the *Due Repulse*, Ralegh in the *Warspite*, both among the newest of Hawkins's creations. As they neared Cadiz, Ralegh, detailed to make a sweep of the shore north of the city, was not present when a council of captains decided on a conventional, old-time plan of attack: the ships would debark Vere's troops to the west of the harbor and send them to take the city; the fleet would then go round and meet the troops in the harbor.

The landing did not take place: heavy surf upended the longboats as they attempted to set the soldiers on the beach. The survivors had to be received back into the ships.

The alternative strategy was direct entry into the harbor. Returning from his sweep, Ralegh initiated a naval engagement that became a brilliant victory. He sailed straight in, ordering music to be played on deck as he went, and the fleet followed. The harbor was guarded by four of the twelve great post-Armada galleons that Philip had named for the Apostles. Vere competed with Ralegh for precedence, even putting a line on the *Warspite* in an effort to draw even. Ralegh cut the line. Selecting the largest Apostle, the 1,500-ton *St. Philip* that had led the attack on Grenville at the Azores, he revenged the *Revenge*. Startled by the unexpected onslaught, the Apostles cut their cables, but without space to maneuver they quickly grounded at the harbor's edge. Their crews spilled over their sides without attempting a defense. Two, the *St. Philip* and the *St. Thomas*, exploded. The unconventional, new-style victory opened the harbor to plunder.

The rest of the raid was an extravagant and undisciplined celebration, at all levels of responsibility. Elizabeth had always been careful not to abase the value of her royal honors by the numbers awarded, but Essex, ever eager to bind men to him by such gifts, and Howard dubbed sixty knights at once, Humphrey Gilbert's son, Ralegh's nephew, among them. Gentlemen, common seamen, and soldiery sacked the town with vigor.

During this orgy, the man whose inventive approach had caused the raid's success lay immobilized in the *Warspite*—a shot had struck Ralegh in the leg. While thus out of action, he developed a further plan. Most of the Spanish merchant fleet, fully loaded, was said to be in the inner harbor, less than a mile away. Early next morning, he sent his newly knighted nephew John and Sir Arthur Throckmorton to the flagship to ask permission for him to push further upstream and capture these lucrative cargoes. A quick advance could have secured them, but Ralegh's colleagues, perhaps still confused by incidental pleasures of the previous evening, fell to quarreling over the ransoms to be demanded of the merchant owners. While the English argued, these gentlemen, foreseeing a foray, agreed to burn their goods rather than lose them to enemy forces. The fire was awesome: cargo worth twelve million ducats went up in smoke. Still too muddled for much regret, the raiders went home to parade their victory.

Though the shot that entered Ralegh's leg at Cadiz forced him to use a cane thereafter, the success of the raid made the next year, 1597, feel rather like old times. On the first of June, Ralegh was received at court, and after long absence resumed his duties as Captain of the Guard.

But there were differences. At sixty-five, Elizabeth was in the eyes of the young men of Essex's generation a faded woman, contemporary with their grandmothers, a figure becoming more and more incongruous as England's royal sovereign. It was inevitable that Essex, in the prime of his young manhood, endowed with the charisma of a political darling and lacking only the gift of judgment and self-control, should look toward a royal succession, which in any case could not be far away, and a part for himself in influencing and perhaps expediting it.

Others were also considering their positions in the realm's future. Except for Elizabeth, practically none of the great figures of her reign were still alive. In 1597, Burghley, who was to live but one more year, was replaced as the queen's principal minister by his younger son, Sir Robert Cecil, and on assuming his father's post Cecil began to fortify his position for the longer term. As the surviving and still-vigorous member of the older generation, Sir Walter Ralegh, restored to Her Majesty's favor, was recognized by the younger men as a still-important factor in the competition for power on the accession of a new ruler. Significantly, when Cecil invited Essex and Ralegh to dinner and the theater in July, the play of the evening was *The Tragedy of Richard II*, Shakespeare's drama of the deposition of a king. Elizabeth is said to have quickly interpreted the meaning of the choice: "Know ye not that I am Richard?"

That same month, two of the three theatergoers took part in the next attack on Spain, known as the "Islands Voyage." On this occasion, Essex replaced Howard, who was in temporary ill health, as Lord Admiral. Ralegh, again in the *Warspite*, was a rear admiral in charge of one of the four squadrons. The 100-sail fleet contained seventeen royal ships, two of which were captured Apostles that had been reconditioned. The plan was to go to Spain, attack and immobilize the Spanish fleet at Ferrol, then turn to intercept the annual treasure fleet at the Azores. But Bay of Biscay storms drove Ralegh and Essex home. On a fresh start, they decided to omit Ferrol and go directly to the Azores. After more storms,

The aged Queen Elizabeth.

Ralegh reached the island of Fayal, where Essex and he had agreed to meet. When Essex did not arrive, Ralegh landed, in violation of previous orders, and took the town. His excuse was that he needed provisions. When Essex did appear on the scene, the insubordination outraged him; Ralegh barely escaped a court-martial. Yet the capture of the town turned out to be the sole positive result of the entire undertaking, for the Spanish *flota* slipped past them to safety in an anchorage so heavily protected that Ralegh and Essex dared not attempt to enter.

In 1598, Ralegh worked hard to get Elizabeth to appoint him to a more substantive post. A dozen possibilities were whispered around the court. What he wanted was what he had always wanted, a seat on the Privy Council, but none was offered. He had to be content with the governorship of the island of Jersey, a strategic location but far from the center of influence.

Essex likewise sought new preferment, and likewise failed to secure his wish. His eye first turned to the lucrative Mastership of the Wards, because as holder of the post he could exert leverage on the nobility, and also because his debts were reaching formidable proportions. Elizabeth not only refused him this, but shortly awarded the plum to Cecil. Changing his objective from civilian influence to the possibility of military glory, Essex then pursued and obtained the office of Lord Deputy in Ireland, where the English position was in jeopardy because of the uprising of Hugh O'Neill, earl of Tyrone, holder of central and eastern Ulster. Tyrone, who had spent considerable time in England, was a formidable antagonist with firm control over his troops.

Essex was given exceptional forces—16,000 foot soldiers and 1,300 horse—and specifically instructed, at a Privy Council meeting with the queen present, to invade and subdue Ulster. In fine fettle, he set forth from London in the spring of 1599, accompanied by many of his own devoted entourage, with two of them, the earl of Southampton and the earl of Devonshire's younger brother, as his major officers. (Since the queen had overtly opposed the naming of Southampton, Essex conferred the title of Master of the Horse only after reaching Ireland.) But he did not attack Ulster. After some desultory campaigning in Leinster and

Memorial engraving of Essex, executed for treason in 1601.

Munster, he returned to Dublin. There, letters from the queen charged him with neglect of orders, and suggested his movements seemed less like a campaign than a progress. Though forbidden to do so, he had continued his lavish distribution of knighthoods. By autumn, his expedition had cost Elizabeth some £300,000 with nothing to show for it. In September, after a token advance against Tyrone, he held a long conference with the rebel, informing him of his future plans; they then made a truce, after which, with many of his companions, Essex returned to London.

Just what those plans comprised can be argued; at the least they envisaged the deposition of the queen, and Essex had been in communication with the expectant James of Scotland. Insubordination had moved into the realm of treason.

The coup that Essex attempted the next February was a failure; his execution occurred on Ash Wednesday, 1601. As Captain of the Guard, Ralegh was required to witness it. His presence on the scaffold was resented by the attending public, for to many of the Londoners who had made Essex their darling, Ralegh now appeared as the surviving rival:

> Ralegh doth time bestride:
> He sits twixt wind and tide:
> Yet uphill he cannot ride,
> For all his bloody pride.

So Ralegh retired to the Armory to observe the headsman's act from a window. His enemies gloated; his friends found him deeply depressed.

The danger to the queen had thus been defused, but in succeeding months, more and more feelers from courtiers and royal advisers continued to slip up the Great North Road to Edinburgh.

Some of the place-seekers sought to strengthen their own prospects by derogating others. Among the most virulent of the aristocrats prepositioning themselves was the poison-tongued Lord Henry Howard, a man who hated Ralegh; he warned James against a coven of atheistic wizards to which Henry Brooke (who had just succeeded his father as Lord Cobham), Henry Percy, duke of Northumberland, and Ralegh were alleged to belong.

Among royal advisers, Robert Cecil was intensely engaged in developing a liaison with the future king comparable to that which his father had managed when Elizabeth succeeded Mary. He had physical disadvantages to overcome: unlike his father, whose stature and serene expression inspired confidence at sight, the hunchbacked Cecil, only a few inches above five feet in height, lacked bodily strength. His crueler detractors rhymed that

> Backed like a lute-case,
> Bellied like a drum,
> Like Jackanapes on horseback
> Sits little Robin Thumb.

But Cecil always knew which way the wind was blowing, and was dexterous at keeping the weather gauge. The oil painting of the Somerset House Conference for making peace with Spain in 1604—the year before James honored him with the earldom of Salisbury—symbolizes his success; seated in the right forefront, he is the United Kingdom's delegation leader. In the late 1590s, by insensible degrees, he changed from Ralegh's friend to his secret enemy. On the surface their good relations remained unbroken; he and Ralegh continued to share interests in ships commissioned against Spain, and after Cecil's wife died in 1591, Bess had foster-mothered Cecil's sickly son William, restoring him to sturdy health in country-fresh air with her family at Sherborne. But Cecil's advice to the incoming monarch was such as to account for James's response when Ralegh was presented to him after his accession: "I have indeed heard rawley of thee."

As soon as Elizabeth died in March 1603, a demolition squad was assigned to the pedestal supporting her former favorite: he was immediately replaced as Captain of the Guard by the Scottish Sir Thomas Erskine. Monopolies he had enjoyed for as much as a quarter-century were allotted to others. By the end of May, the Raleghs had been given three weeks to get out of Durham House. Only Sherborne seemed secure: in 1599 Ralegh had received a grant in perpetuity to the property, and in 1602 he had transferred it to Wat by a formal deed.

Then in mid-July, the statue itself was taken down. At Windsor, where Ralegh had gone to take part in a royal hunt, Cecil informed him that the king wished him to stay behind for interrogation by the Privy Council. A conspiracy against the king, headed by Lord Cobham and the Spanish ambassador to the Spanish Netherlands, had been unmasked, and Ralegh was thought to have had knowledge of it. Within a week he was in the Tower, accused of high treason.

Two plots figured in the charges against him: the "Bye" plot, instigated by two Catholic priests, and the "Main" plot, in which some of Ralegh's associates aimed to supplant James with another Scottish claimant, his cousin Arabella Stuart. Through an emissary in the Tower, Ralegh was able to request Cobham to write a letter exonerating him from complicity; after a first draft that Ralegh found unsatisfactory, Cobham supplied a second letter, on which Ralegh relied, not knowing that Cobham had promptly revealed Ralegh's correspondence to the Council. Ralegh was also depending on a second false reliance: though formerly the law had required two witnesses in support of testimony in cases such as his, a recent revision had reduced the requirement to one.

Since plague was carrying off two thousand Londoners a week that year, the royal court and the legal courts prudently left the city; Ralegh's trial was moved to Winchester, with a Middlesex jury brought down to hear it. At the same time, an eleven-man commission had been empaneled. Four members were justices familiar with the law, Lord Chief Justice Popham among them; of the remaining seven, three had already been awarded peerages in the seven months that James had been king, and three others were about to be so elevated; the seventh was William Waad, clerk of the Privy Council and soon to be Lieutenant of the Tower. All except Waad held either court offices or appointments to the Privy Council. With the verdict thus assured in advance, the case was a pure formality.

There were five charges:

1. At Durham House, Ralegh had engaged in a conspiracy to put Arabella Stuart on James's throne—she would then sign a peace with Spain and tolerate Catholicism in England.

With confidence restored, Sir Robert Cecil appears as head of the United Kingdom delegation at the Somerset House Conference in 1604. Behind him, on the right, sit other successful courtiers: Henry Howard, newly created earl of Northampton; Charles Blount, earl of Devonshire; Charles Howard, earl of Effingham under Elizabeth, now first earl of Nottingham under James; and Thomas Sackville, earl of Dorset. Among the Spanish, the fourth from the front is the Count Aremberg, Spanish ambassador to the Spanish Netherlands, who figured in James I's treatment of Ralegh.

2. Lord Cobham and his brother George Brooke had in Ralegh's presence used the phrase "there would never be a good world in England until the king and his cubs are taken away," and Ralegh had not reported it.

3. Ralegh had stimulated Cobham to treason with a book that denied James's claim.

4. He had incited Brooke to initiate negotiations between Arabella and Philip.

5. He had urged Cobham to obtain 600,000 crowns from Count Aremberg, Spanish ambassador to the Spanish Netherlands.

The prosecutor was the attorney general, Sir Edward Coke. Under the law, a defendant on a charge of treason was not entitled to counsel, or to give evidence under oath; he could do no more than offer explanatory statements. Coke, now in his tenth year as attorney general, was a different man as prosecutor from what he was in his later years as a judge and defender of the rights of Englishmen against the Stuart prerogative. As prosecutor, his style was to bully the prisoner, prejudice the jury by statements not relevant to the case, and curry favor with the Crown. His words, threateningly uttered to an average prisoner awed by the panoply of the law and the Latin phrases interjected into its citation, were usually effective. But not when directed against a prisoner like Ralegh, well able to trade Latin for Latin, and not in a case where bluster only partially veiled a lack of evidence.

Ralegh had never been a popular figure. Because he was a commoner like themselves, the splendor to which he rose under Elizabeth had set the little green worm of envy chewing on the London mobs who loved a lord enough to forgive him an exalted status. He had been called "the best hated man in England," and William Waad, who had been in charge of his transfer from the Tower to Winchester's Wolvesey Castle, told Cecil that it was "hob or nob whether or not Ralegh should have been brought alive through such multitudes of unruly people as did exclaim against him." So when Coke began his castigation, Ralegh stood at the bar without sympathy. When he stepped down, the court having done its predetermined duty, he was a convicted traitor, condemned to

King James I.

die under the medieval formula: to be hanged, but cut down while still alive; to be drawn, with his heart and bowels cut from his body; and his body then to be quartered. (The quarters were usually exhibited at the town gates.) Yet by the end of that long day, the public appreciation of Ralegh had been transformed. The quality of his responses to Coke's rabid allegations, the calm of his demeanor in his requests for evidence and for witnesses and for consideration of the likelihood of complicity with Spain in view of his entire life's record, had given the nation a new hero.

Coke, in order to recall past affirmations that Ralegh was an atheist, had begun by referring to the "Bye" plot, with regard to which the prisoner had not been charged at all. When he turned to the actual charges, Ralegh said, "Your words cannot condemn me; my innocence is my defence; prove one of those things wherewith you have charged me, and I will confess the whole indictment, and that I am the most horrible traitor that ever lived, and worthy to be crucified with a thousand torments." Coke's reply was, "Nay, I will prove all; thou art a monster, thou hast an English face, but a Spanish heart."

A little later, Ralegh: "I do not hear yet that you have spoken one word against me; here is no treason of mine done. If my Lord Cobham be a traitor, what is that to me?"

Coke: "All that he did was by thy instigation, thou viper; 'twas through thee, thou traitor."

Ralegh: "It becometh not a man of quality and virtue to call me so; but I take comfort in it, it is all you can do."

Perhaps most telling of all was the exchange when Ralegh asked for the production of witnesses.

Ralegh: "You try me by the Spanish inquisition, if you proceed only by the circumstances without two witnesses."

Coke: "This is a treasonable speech."

Ralegh: ". . . It is no rare thing for a man to be falsely accused. My lords, it is not against nor contrary to law to have my accuser brought hither; I do not demand it of right, and yet I must needs tell you, that

Sir Edward Coke, prosecutor in Ralegh's trial in 1603.

you will deal very severely with me if you condemn me, and not bring my accuser to my face."

But that was exactly what they did. The prisoner was returned to the Tower. In view of public sentiment, James could hardly risk having the sentence carried out at that time; it was in fact deferred for fifteen years, and the final instrument was not the hangman's rope but the headsman's axe.

Ralegh's life in confinement was not too rigorous. He had two rooms in the Bloody Tower: one looking out to the Thames over the entrance to the Traitors Gate; the other providing a view of Tower Green, where he walked for exercise. He had his own furniture and, best of all, books. (Some of the volumes he had at hand sustained his interest in American settlement: a list of his collection in the Tower starts with a *Planting of Virginia*; in August of the previous year, 1602, he had written Cecil, "I shall yet live to see it an English nation.") Before long, he was permitted to convert a disused chicken house into a tiny laboratory for chemical experiments. He kept servants, and depending on the good will of the Tower's current lieutenant, he received visitors; Bess, with Wat, lived for a time within the Tower walls, and in 1605 their son Carew was born and baptised there. Under some wardens, Ralegh dined from time to time at their table; under others, a five o'clock curfew evicted visitors, and Bess had to take lodgings in the neighborhood. In spite of the Tower's dampness, Ralegh kept well, though in 1606 he seems to have experienced a stroke from which he soon recovered.

Some of his experiments in the chicken coop evolved into medicines. A chance visit from the French ambassadress introduced his Guiana Balsam to her, and having tested its virtues she made it known to James's queen, Anne of Denmark, who sent for a bottle, came to visit its maker, and subsequently brought her kingly father to meet him.

It was through James's queen that by 1608 Ralegh had a firm relationship as an informal counselor and mentor to her eldest son, Henry, Prince of Wales, a promising fourteen-year-old with a thorough distaste for his father's corrupt court. A manly boy, both outdoorsman and student, he read with avidity the papers Ralegh wrote for him on shipbuilding and

S fees patris et sophiæ fatoeum
    lege perenitus
Ante diem, lachrimas et inana
    vota relinquo

Hee that the LIFE of this FACE euer saw
The MILDNES in it noting, and the AVE
Will iudgethat PEACE, did either in hir LOUE
So soone aduance hem to hir STATE aboue

Or else in FEARE that HEE would WAR Bi preserue
Concluded with HIM HEE should LIVE with
To both, HIS agines sluethie afeares ;
In eurie SOLDIER s greise SCHOLLEE S tures

The Stuart Prince Henry, heir apparent to King James I.

sea-service, and incorporated much of the advice he received into the building of the *Prince Royal* in 1612. (Ralegh's own former ship, the *Ark Ralegh*, which as the *Ark Royal* had led the English ships against the Armada, was rebuilt at this time and named *Anne Royal* for the queen.) Prince Henry likewise concerned himself with the renewal of American colonization by the Virginia Company: at its first fleet's landfall in 1607, at Chesapeake Bay, the bay's southern point had been named Cape Henry in his honor.

It was for the prince that Ralegh began his major prose work, projected as a history of the world, an account of human society from its beginning to the present, with an ethical analysis of the merits of successive kings.

As of 1612, it looked as though this young heir to the English throne might one day place Ralegh in his court as a chief member of the Privy Council on which Ralegh had longed to serve under the great queen. Henry had said, "No king but my father would keep such a bird in a cage."

The two also collaborated in respect to their private affairs. James had a design for marrying his eldest son and his daughter Elizabeth to a princess and prince of the small Catholic state of Savoy; Ralegh wrote a paper against the project. When one of the king's beautiful favorites, Robert Carr, cast his eye on Sherborne, Henry intervened. Wat Ralegh's title was faulty; his father had not proofread the deed by which he transferred it, and the clerk-copyist must have been interrupted in his work, for he omitted the key phrase of the transfer, that Wat "shall and will from henceforth stand and be thereof seised." Since Ralegh could do nothing—a convicted traitor was dead to the law—Henry contrived to get the property put in his own name, and the death in May 1612 of Robert Cecil—Lord Salisbury since 1605—removed the greatest bar to Ralegh's release and enjoyment of it.

But these, the best of Ralegh's last years, were brought to an abrupt end that autumn. Prince Henry went swimming in the polluted Thames; a few weeks later—though some of Ralegh's elixir was sent for at the last moment—he died of typhoid fever.

Ralegh stopped work on his *History*. The first volume, covering the years to 168 B.C., came out unsigned in 1614 and was so immediately popular that James attempted to suppress it. With its strictures on evil kings, the book became a source for Puritans in the coming Civil War. By the mid-seventeenth century, the central political issue in England was the responsibility of monarchs: were they kings by divine right, authorized by God to be the final interpreters of the law, as the Stuarts insisted, or were they as well as their subjects bound to live under the law and be governed by it? Milton greatly admired the *History*, and Cromwell and Lilburne read into its pages their justification as regicides. For the overriding question of their time, Ralegh had written a textbook.

Then in 1616, the Tower's portcullis unexpectedly rose for Ralegh's exit. His release was conditional, but it brought momentary freedom. Its cause: James needed money. The king's military expenses had been minimal. The wars were over. A comprehensive peace with Spain had been signed in the second year of his reign—he was currently negotiating a marriage between the Spanish infanta and Prince Charles, his new heir apparent. For the time being, Ireland was quiet. But, rather than diminishing, his debts had been mounting, and by the time of Ralegh's release they topped £700,000.

Since stopping work on his *History*, Ralegh had reverted, with increased interest, to his long preoccupation with Guiana: the king might find it profitable to give him freedom to search for the great gold mine. Yet he had no precise idea of where it was.

The project was delicate, for James was close to becoming the creature of Spain's ambassador in London since 1613, Don Diego Sarmiento de Acuña, Count Gondomar. The king had even made him an adviser to his Privy Council as well as his confidante. Gondomar had a special antagonism to Ralegh, for Ralegh had once captured and held prisoner his relative Pedro Sarmiento de Gamboa, the man who had told Ralegh of the gold of El Dorado.

Lest Spain take Ralegh's arrival as a trespass, James supplied Gondomar with exact information about the ships of Ralegh's fleet, their intended course, and their instructions for their exploration, including a

Ralegh's *History of the World* was published anonymously in 1614; the author was, after all, a prisoner convicted of treason. The allegorical frontispiece of the first edition was designed to convey the work's purpose: Under the allseeing eye of Providence, a tall figure representing History, the Mistress of Man's Life, holds up a globe showing the continents of Europe, Africa, and the Americas, with busy shipping in the North Atlantic. To the left and right of the globe, winged figures of Good Fame and Ill Fame trumpet their news. To the right of History, at whose feet are Death and Oblivion, is a beautiful woman, Truth, standing between pillars labeled the Life of Memory and the Light of Truth; to her left, an aged crone, between pillars labeled the Message of Antiquity and the Witness of Time, holds a plumb-line and represents Experience.

When the next edition of Ralegh's *History* came out in 1617, King James had released the author from the Tower to search for Guiana gold, and the title page bore not only Ralegh's name but also his portrait engraved by the artist Simon van de Passe.

THE
HISTORIE OF
THE VVORLD.

IN FIVE BOOKES.

1.   Ntreating of the Beginning and firſt Ages of the ſame from the Creation vnto Abraham.
2.   Of the Times from the Birth of Abraham, to the deſtruction of the Temple of Salomon.
3.   From the deſtruction of Ieruſalem, to the time of Philip of Macedon.
4.   From the Reigne of Philip of Macedon, to the eſtabliſhing of that King-dome, in the Race of Antigonus.
5.   From the ſettled rule of Alexanders ſucceſſours in the Eaſt, vntill the Ro-mans (preuailing ouer all) made Conqueſt of Aſia and Macedon.

By Sir WALTERRALEGH, Knight.

VERA EFFIGIES CLARISSᴬᴬᴵ VIRI DOM· IN GVALTHERI RALEGH EQV. AUR. et

The true and lively portraiture of the honourable and learned Knight Sʳ Walter Ralegh

AMORE ET VIRTVTE

strict ban on any conflict with Spanish settlements. The delighted ambassador sent these home to be read and forwarded to the West Indies. Gondomar also received a message that "His Majesty is very disposed and determined against Ralegh, and will join the king of Spain in ruining him, but he wishes this resolution to be kept secret for the moment at least."

Before starting, Ralegh, suspecting much, had taken his own precautions. If his expedition were a failure, he knew that the carrying out of his sentence would not be long delayed. From the French envoy in London he obtained a privateering commission that would justify any captures he might make, and offer French haven to him on his return if needed.

The departure of Ralegh's fleet from Plymouth on June 12, 1617, was feted as in old times, but it received a sorry send-off from the weather. On their third try, the ships got out of the Channel, only to be forced to take refuge in Cork. By the time they reached the Canaries, sickness had begun to weaken the crews: the *Destiny*, Ralegh's flagship, lost more than two-score men during the transatlantic crossing. Ralegh himself was flat on his back for a month, and arrived too weak to take part in the advance up the Orinoco. Lawrence Keymiss, the Oxford don who had been on the 1595 voyage and returned for a further reconnaissance thereafter, replaced him as leader.

But where was the leader to go? Previous exploration by others had dissipated belief in the existence of Manoa and its gilded king, and the location of the mine was composed only of conjecture. The worst happened when Keymiss, after much wandering, camped near the Spanish town of San Thomé in hopes of picking up clues. The Spaniards attacked his camp, and young Wat Ralegh, eager for glory, led and died in a counterattack that took the town and killed the Spanish governor. Recognizing the full implications of the expedition's failure, Keymiss returned to the ships. After being fiercely upbraided by Ralegh, he retired to his cabin and killed himself.

In a letter to Bess breaking the news of Wat's death, Ralegh accepted the completeness of the disaster: "I never knew sorrow until now. . . .

Don Diego Sarmiento de Acuña, Count Gondomar, Spanish ambassador
to London, 1613–18 and 1619–22.

Comfort your heart (dearest Bess) I shall sorrow for us both. I shall sorrow the less, because I have not long to sorrow, because not long to live."

On June 21, 1618, the *Destiny* reached Plymouth. Ralegh had expected immediate arrest, but Sir Lewis Stukeley, Vice Admiral of Devon and a Ralegh relative, left him free; reunited with Bess, he considered his predicament.

Though the king saw little of his queen, and cared less, Ralegh petitioned her for intercession:

> O had Truth Power the guiltlesse could not fall
> Malice winne Glorie, or Revenge triumphe;
> But Truth alone can not encounter all . . .
>
> All love and all desert of former tymes
> Malice hath covered from my Soveraignes Eies,
> And largelie laid abroad supposed crimes . . .
>
> Then unto whom shall I unfold my wrong,
> Cast downe my teares or hold up folded hands?
> To her to whom remorse doth most belong.

The king was undergoing perplexities of his own. Gondomar's tour of duty was to end in July: perhaps postponement of a decision until after he left would make it appear less dictated. Gondomar's demand for a special meeting of the Privy Council had increased James's problems: when the diplomat there revealed the king's promise to send Ralegh to Spain for such disposition as Philip III might find suitable, even complaisant Francis Bacon, James's Lord Chancellor, newly ennobled as Lord Verulam, Viscount St. Albans, objected to the transfer of an English subject for punishment by a foreign sovereign. Yet in spite of Council disapproval, James repeated his offer in writing as Gondomar left for home, and told the Council that he considered it to have made a unanimous decision against Ralegh and would treat as treasonable any denial. Sir Lewis Stukeley was then ordered to arrest Ralegh and bring him to London.

Meanwhile, Ralegh was vacillating from plan to plan. One option was to fly to France—one of his old Plymouth captains was willing to row him out to a waiting ship. Twice, Ralegh decided to go; twice, at the last moment, he chose to return to shore. On the way to London, he attempted to gain time to write an apologia for the expedition to Guiana by feigning elaborate sickness, aided by drugs provided by a French physician. When this interruption of his trip was over, he was surprised at being permitted to go to Bess's lodgings instead of being confined to the Tower. The permission was given because Stukeley had learned that she and the Plymouth captain were continuing to collude; he had set spies to watch their movements. Their plan turned into a ghastly farce when Sir Walter, in crude disguise and accompanied by Stukeley, in whom he had confided, was rowed down the Thames into prearranged custody awaiting him at Greenwich. (Thereafter, Stukeley was popularly known as Sir Judas.) For the final time, Ralegh was then returned to the Tower.

The king's legal counsel, Bacon and Coke, found grounds for justifying execution hard to come by. There was even the possibility that James's commission to Ralegh to lead the Guiana expedition had constituted a pardon, since it gave Ralegh power over English subjects. But time pressed; word arrived from Spain that Philip III would leave Ralegh's punishment to James after all, but wished execution to take place within the month if negotiations for Prince Charles's marriage were to proceed smoothly. James's advisers could suggest nothing more promising than reliance on the old verdict of 1603, embellished with a statement derogating Ralegh's late behavior, or else the finding of a new verdict by carefully selected noblemen at a hearing where Ralegh could make a reply before being condemned. Remembering Winchester, "where by his wit he turned the hatred of men into compassion for him," James opted for a hearing in camera, with execution to be followed by a published declaration of its cause. A hearing was duly held, with Bacon delivering the sentence.

But the law officers who received the warrant did not think that reaffirmation of a fifteen-year-old authorization was adequate; they held that a current condemnation by the Court of King's Bench was required. So on October 28, 1618, Ralegh was brought across the city from the Tower to Westminster Hall.

Though its result was the same, the tone of the proceeding was very different from that at Winchester: the new Lord Chief Justice, Sir Henry Montague, erased one of Lord Popham's slanders and paid tribute to Ralegh's *History* when he said, "Your faith hath heretofore been questioned, but I am resolved you are a good Christian; for your book, which is an admirable work, doth testify as much." And Henry Yelverton, Coke's successor as attorney general, said in his summing up: "Sir Walter Ralegh hath been a statesman, and a man, who, in regard to his parts and quality, is to be pitied. He hath been as a star at which the world hath gazed; but stars may fall; nay, they must fall when they trouble the sphere wherein they abide. It is, therefore, his majesty's pleasure now to call for execution of the former judgment, and I now require order for the same." (Bacon, in his essays, had written that judges should be lions, but lions under the throne. As the seventeenth century moved on, the Stuarts could have noticed that the lions were growling.) The only change in the determination of Ralegh's fate was that, in accordance with a warrant issued by the king, he was to be beheaded rather than made to suffer the gross indignity of being hanged, drawn, and quartered.

Procedure completed, the execution was set for the next morning. The condemned man was to spend the night in the Abbey Gatehouse, while a scaffold was erected in the Old Palace Yard.

The first hours of Ralegh's last night turned into a reception for his many friends. When some of them worried at the lightness of his mood, he quipped, "It is my last mirth in this world—do not grudge it to me," and then added the double pun: "When I come to the sad parting, you will find me grave enough."

Later, he and Bess said goodbye, after close to thirty years of shared courage. (To one of the evenings's guests, Ralegh had given the epigram: "Cowards fear to die, but Courage stout / Rather than live in snuff, will be put out.") At midnight, when the Carews led Bess away, she said she had been told that she was to be given his body. He replied, "It is well, dear Bess, that thou mayst dispose of that dead which thou hadst not always the disposing of when alive."

Later in the night, on a leaf of his Bible, Ralegh changed the opening and added two lines to the last verse of the poem he had written to this woman at their first love:

> Even such is tyme which takes in trust
> Our yowth, our Joyes and all we have,
> And payes us butt with age and dust:
> Who in the darke and silent grave
> When we have wandred all our wayes
> Shutts up the storye of our dayes.
> And from which earth and grave and dust
> The Lord shall rayse me up I trust.

At dawn, when the dean of Westminster, Dr. Robert Touson, brought the sacrament for Ralegh's last communion, he found him "very cheerful and merry." The day before, he had left the Tower with his white hair unkempt, and bantered with a serving man who offered to comb it, "Let them kem it that are to have it," but this morning, he dressed with his old fastidious care: ash-colored silk stockings, black knee breeches, an embroidered waistcoat, a black doublet, and, over all, a black velvet coat—it was a chilly October morning. He ate a good breakfast, enjoyed a last smoke, and as he left the Gatehouse accepted a cup of sack, replying to the donor, "I will answer you as did the fellow who drank of St. Giles's bowl as he went to Tyburn: 'It's a good drink, if a man might but tarry by it.'"

Always, Ralegh had been something of an actor; and during the small hours prior to the execution he may have rehearsed the lines of his farewell performance. When he mounted the scaffold it was in the role of the Renaissance Man, advancing to take the curtain call on the Elizabethan drama and to say a final word on behalf of the company.

A close-packed audience awaited it. The night before, when Sir Hugh

Portrait engraving of Sir Walter Ralegh, with a sketch of his execution below.

Beeston had mentioned his intention of attendance on the morrow, Ralegh had bantered: "I do not know what you may do for a place. For my own part, I am sure of one. You must make what shift you can."

As Ralegh began to speak, nobles in the windows overlooking the courtyard could not hear; the earls of Arundel, Oxford, and Northampton joined him on the scaffold. James, as John Aubrey noted, had hoped to contrive a thin attendance by setting the execution on London's Lord Mayor's Day, when "the pageants and fine shows might draw away the people from beholding the tragedy of one of the gallantest worthies that ever England bred."

Past and future were present: in the crowd were men—John Hampden, John Pym—who over the next twenty years were to bring on the Puritan Revolution; John Eliot, until then a follower of James's favorite, George Villiers, duke of Buckingham, was turned into an anti-monarchist by the events of this day.

When the headsman cleared the scaffold, Ralegh stood alone at center stage and spoke, denying one by one the charges brought against him. Then, moving downstage to the scaffold's edge, he asked the crowd to pray with him "to the great God of Heaven whom I have grievously offended. . . . For a long time my course was a course of vanity. I have been a seafaring man, a soldier, and a courtier, and in the temptation of the least of these there is enough to overthrow a good mind and a good man. So I take my leave of you all, making my peace with God. I have a long journey to make and must bid the company farewell."

Here, on the scaffold, he was the last of the confraternity of great Devon captains of the ocean. For over three decades, carrying the English flag, they had encompassed the world. The great queen whom they had served had like himself survived them, yet she too had been in her grave for what was approaching a generation. He alone was left, and none would be left tomorrow. The cold autumn wind ruffled his white hair as he took off his coat and his doublet.

Ralegh asked the executioner to let him see the axe, and tested the blade with a finger: "This is a sharp medicine, but it is a sure cure for all diseases." The executioner spread his own cloak before Ralegh, and knelt to make the customary request for the victim's forgiveness. Ralegh put his hands on the man's shoulders: "When I stretch forth my hands, despatch me."

In the crowd, someone asked if he did not want to die facing east towards Jerusalem. "So the heart be right," came the response, "it is no matter which way the head lieth." He refused a blindfold: "Think you I fear the shadow of the axe, when I fear not the axe itself?"

He placed his head on the block, prayed for a moment, then stretched out his hands. The headsman was too moved to move. Again, the outstretched hands; again, no movement. Then, a sharp command: "What do you fear? Strike, man, strike!"

On the second stroke, the head split from the body. Silently, the headsman held it up; the groan from the crowd forbade him the words that usually accompanied this gesture: "Behold, the head of a traitor!"

Instead, a voice from the multitude below the scaffold countered: "We have not another such head to be cut off!"

In the hush that followed, the curtain of time closed on the Elizabethan era.

Notes to the Illustrations

Notes to the Illustrations

Several museums and libraries have been especially generous in supplying photographs for illustrations in this book. In the notes, the following abbreviated identifications serve to acknowledge permission and copyright:

BM: By permission of the Trustees of the British Museum, London

Folger: By permission of the Folger Shakespeare Library, Washington, D.C.

NPG: National Portrait Gallery, London

The majority of the illustrations related to the Spanish Armada of 1588 come from one source, which deserves particular mention.

When the English fleet returned from the Armada encounter, Charles Howard, Lord High Admiral, summoned Robert Adams, Surveyor of the Queen's Buildings, and after describing each day's location and events as the Armada swept up the Channel and into the North Sea, commissioned him to prepare drawings based on this account. From them, Augustine Ryther engraved "Tables" and in 1590 published them along with a translation of P. Ubaldini's *Expeditionis Hispanorum in Angliam Vera Descriptio* under the title *A Discours concerninge the Spanish fleete inuadinge Englande in the yeare 1588*. On the basis of these "Tables" the Flemish tapissier Henry Cornelius Vroom designed for Lord Howard a series of tapestries depicting the entire encounter. To the surprise of the Court, Howard did not present them to Queen Elizabeth; after her death he sold them to King James I, who had them hung in the House of Lords. They remained there until they were destroyed in the catastrophic fire of the nineteenth century. In 1739, however, the engraver John Pine had preserved their likeness in his *Tapestry Hangings of the House of Lords, representing the several engagements between the English and Spanish fleets in the ever memorable year 1588*. It is from this source that the illustrations of the Armada used in this book have been taken, with the kind permission of the Folger Shakespeare Library. The citation given is "Pine," followed by the plate number, if marked, as well as the pencilled number on the page in the Folger's copy of the volume (cat. listing: DA1739.360.P4, cage).

Frontispiece: Oil by George Gower, in the collection at Woburn Abbey. By kind permission of the Marquess of Tavistock and the Trustees of the Bedford Estates.

p. xii: Pine, plate I of page pencilled no. 1.

p. 3: Pine, plate IV of page pencilled no. 2.

p. 5: John Huighen van Linschoten, *Itinerario* (1598), between pp. 32–33. Folger. Cat. listing: STC 15691.

p. 11: BM, Prints and Drawings. Cat. listing: Royal Portraits, 1976 u 25.

p. 15: John Nichols, *Progresses and Processions of Queen Elizabeth* (1788–1805), vol. 3, facing p. 101. Folger. Cat. listing: DA356.E7, cage.

p. 19: Engraving by George Vertue, 1735, from an oil portrait by Titian, in *The History of England, written in French by Paul Rapin de Thoyras, translated into English with additional notes by N. Tindal, M.A., rector of Halverstoke in Hampshire, and chaplain to the Royal Hospital at Greenwich* (3d edition, 1743), vol. 2, p. 37. Courtesy of The Mariners Museum, Newport News, Virginia.

p. 20: Willem Janszoon Blaeu, *The Light of Nauigation* (1622), frontispiece. Folger. Cat. listing: STC 3112.

p. 22: Cotton Augustus, I, 1, f. 41. Courtesy of the Trustees of the British Library, London.

p. 27: The Anthony Roll, Pepysian Library, Magdalene College, Cambridge. By permission of the Master and Fellows, Magdalene College, Cambridge.

p. 34: Pine, cartouche from plate V of page pencilled no. 11.

p. 36: Oil portrait on panel, by Hieronimo Custodis of Antwerp. In the collection at Buckland Abbey. By permission of the Plymouth City Museum and Art Gallery.

p. 39, top: *Fragments of Ancient English Shipwrightry* (c. 1586–1630), Ms. 2820, Pepysian Library, Magdalene College, Cam-

bridge. By permission of the Master and Fellows of Magdalene College, Cambridge.

p. 39, bottom: Source and credit as for the preceding illustration.

p. 41: Source and credit as for the preceding illustration.

p. 47: Engraving from Henry Holland, *Herωologia Anglica* (1620), facing p. 100. Folger. Cat. listing: STC 13582, copy 1.

p. 52: Fredericus de Wit, *Poli Artici et circumia centrum terrarum descriptio novissima*, Amsterdam (c. 1690). Courtesy of the Library of Congress, Geography and Map Division.

p. 54: Engraving from Holland, *Herωologia Anglica*, facing p. 97. Folger.

p. 55: Engraving from Rev. Daniel and Samuel Lysons, *Magna Brittania* (1806–22), vol. 6, plate 19, following p. cccxlvi. Folger. Cat. listing: DA625.L9.

p. 57: Oil portrait by an unknown artist, in the collection at Compton Castle. By kind permission of Mr. Geoffrey Gilbert.

p. 67: John Davis, *Seaman's Secrets* (1626 ed.), part 2, E5 recto. Folger. Cat. listing: STC 6370.

p. 68: Willem and Joannis Blaeu, *Theatrum Orbis Terrarum sive Novus Atlas*, fifth part. Sancroft Library, Emmanuel College, Cambridge. By permission of the Master and Fellows of Emmanuel College.

p. 73: Oil portrait by an unknown artist. NPG. Reg. No. 1612.

p. 75, top: Rev. Thomas Moore, *History of Devonshire* (1831), vol. 1, book 4, in series of engravings following p. 574. Courtesy of the Library of Congress. Cat. listing: DA670.D5.M8.

p. 75, bottom: Courtesy of the *Western Morning News*, Plymouth, England.

p. 78: The National Maritime Museum, London.

p. 79: Engraving from Holland, *Herωologia Anglica*, facing p. 88. Folger.

p. 81: Watercolor by John White. Reproduced from the Page-Holgate facsimiles of the American Drawings of John White, the North Carolina Collection of the Wilson Library of the University of North Carolina at Chapel Hill. By permission of the University of North Carolina Press.

p. 83: Source and credit as for preceding illustration.

p. 87: Courtesy of The John Carter Brown Library at Brown University.

p. 93: Engraving by Jodocus Hondius. NPG. Reg. No. 3905.

p. 94: Auguste de Zarate, *Discoverie and Conquest of the Provinces of Peru* (1581), frontispiece. Folger. Cat. listing: STC 26123.

p. 100: Manuscript map showing Drake's route of circumnavigation (London, 1587). Courtesy of the Yale Center for British Art, Paul Mellon Collection. Cat. no.: Map W 1587 (F°B).

p. 102: Engraving by Levinus Hulsius (1603) of the capture of the *Cacafuego*. Rare Books and Manuscripts Division, The New York Public Library, Astor, Lenox and Tilden Foundations.

p. 107: Made in the mid-1590s by the master silversmith Abraham Gessner of Zurich. By permission of the Plymouth City Museum and Art Gallery.

p. 115: Pine, plate II of page pencilled no. 1.

p. 117: Courtesy of The Mariners Museum, Newport News, Virginia.

p. 119: BM, Prints and Drawings.

p. 124: Pine, plate V of page pencilled no. 11.

p. 126: Pine, plate IV of page pencilled no. 10.

p. 129: Pine, plates V and VI of page pencilled no. 3.

p. 132: Pine, plate IX of page pencilled no. 15.

p. 134: Pine, plates IX and X of page pencilled no. 5.

p. 136: Pine, no plate no., page pencilled no. 6.

p. 139: Pine, no plate no., page pencilled no. 18.

p. 140: By permission of the Trustees of the British Library, London. Cat. listing: Coins and Medals, MI 154.

p. 143: MS Rawl. A. 192. Bodleian Library, Oxford.

p. 149: In the collection at Buckland Abbey. By permission of the Plymouth City Museum and Art Gallery.

p. 153: Miniature by Nicholas Hilliard. NPG. Reg. No. 4106.

p. 155: Miniature by Nicholas Hilliard. NPG. Reg. No. 4197.

p. 159: From Robert Wilkinson, *London Illustrata* (London, 1819), plate 99. BM.

p. 161: Engraving by Francis Delaram. BM, Prints and Drawings. Cat. listing: P.1−216.

p. 163: Oil portrait by Mark Gheeraerts the Younger (c. 1592). NPG. Reg. No. 2561.

p. 164: Engraving by George Vertue (1735), from an oil portrait by an unknown artist (c. 1595) now in the Government Art Collection (U.K.) and usually displayed in the Bloody Tower, Tower of London. Cat. listing: LE2791. Courtesy of The Mariners Museum, Newport News, Virginia.

p. 167: BM, Prints and Drawings. Cat. listing: O.7.293.

p. 171: Oil portrait by an unknown artist of the English school. Courtesy of the National Gallery of Ireland, Dublin.

p. 173: Johannes Kip, *Brittania Illustrata, or Views of the royal houses and most noted houses* (1764), plate 7. Folger. Cat. listing: NA7620.K9.1764, cage.

p. 177: Oil portrait by an unknown artist. NPG. Reg. No. 3914.

p. 181: Oil by Mark Gheeraerts after J. Oliver. From The Methuen Collection at Corsham Court. By kind permission of the Lord Methuen.

p. 183: Engraving by Jacobus Houbraken, *Heads of Illustrious Persons of Great Britain* (1743−52), vol. 1, p. 51. Folger. Cat. listing: N7598.H8, cage.

p. 187: NPG. Reg. No. 665.

p. 189: Oil portrait by Daniel Mytens. NPG. Reg. No. 109.

p. 191: Oil portrait by Paul van Somer, in the collection of the Inner Temple. Photo by the Courtauld Institute of Art. By permission of the Masters of the Bench of the Inner Temple.

p. 193: From Holland, *Herωologia Anglica*, facing p. 48. Folger.

p. 197: Folger. Cat. listing: STC 20637.

p. 199: Folger. Cat. listing: STC 20638.

p. 201: BM, Prints and Drawings. Cat. listing: Spanish Portraits.

p. 206: BM, Prints and Drawings. Cat. listing: No. C III Pi 1928-12-10-307.

Index

Index